# The Children
## of Witches

## About the author

Sherri Smith lives in Winnipeg, Canada, where she teaches at a school for children with special needs. *The Children of Witches* is her second novel.

## Also by Sherri Smith

*The Virgin's Tale*

# The Children of Witches

SHERRI SMITH

SIMON &
SCHUSTER

London · New York · Sydney · Toronto

A CBS COMPANY

First published in Great Britain by Simon & Schuster UK Ltd, 2010
A CBS COMPANY

Copyright © Sherri Smith, 2010

1 3 5 7 9 10 8 6 4 2

Simon & Schuster UK Ltd
1st Floor
222 Gray's Inn Road
London WC1X 8HB

www.simonandschuster.co.uk

Simon & Schuster Australia
Sydney

A CIP catalogue record for this book is available
from the British Library

ISBN: 978-1-84737-187-4

Typeset in Plantin by M Rules
Printed in the UK by CPI Mackays, Chatham ME5 8TD

To my parents, Al and Carole Smith
and
grandmother, Grace Graham

As Freud argues in *Totem and Taboo*, the practice of cannibalism can be a kind of intense identification, a type of primary love where attachment is guaranteed by literally incorporating a piece of the other. He suggests there is a cannibalistic component in the fierce love children bear their parents, wanting to consume and replace them utterly.

– Lyndal Roper, *Witch Craze*

Between the dark and the daylight,
   When the night is beginning to lower,
Comes a pause in the day's occupations,
   That is known as the Children's Hour.

– Henry Wadsworth Longfellow
'The Children's Hour'

# PROLOGUE

*Late summer, 1665*

To say the children of Flusstal had run amok in the year 1665 was a grave understatement. To think the children were only wayward and disobedient and in need of some basic discipline and religion, that to spend their daylight hours on Bible study would have turned them right again, was also too slight an assertion. How did such a malign affliction, it was the only word Anna could think of for the omniscient influence the children had fallen under, pass through the city walls so unnoticeably, so soundlessly, as if it had simply been carried on the wind like dandelion snow to fall into the children's mouths and germinate within them.

At which point in time could one say, 'Yes, this was the beginning, this was where and when things began to go terribly wrong.' Anna's outings around the city were always accompanied by a sense of incredulity: how had this happened here? Could it all have been prevented? Useless questions, except to provide her with a feeling of absolution regarding her own lack of action in those early days when prevention had been possible. But how could she have known then what she knew now?

She shifted the basket she was carrying. It held nothing but gave her the appearance that she was out to place orders and make purchases; it gave her something to look busy with.

Above her loomed a black cloud of smoke billowing up against the cobalt sky. It furled and unfurled on itself, and at times had the shape of a large decrepit and gnarled human body rising into the atmosphere which appeared to pace back and forth, as if unsure what to do next. The smoke carried with it a gut-retching odour that was never to entirely dissipate, but remain faintly detectable in the city for years to come. This stench could never be justly described but only given oblique comparisons – a cloying mixture of metal, grease, sulphur, musk and leather. There were moments when Anna caught a scent that smelled specifically like someone: the metallic mushroom aroma was reminiscent of the blacksmith, traces of damp leather reminded her of the shoemaker, and, reluctantly, of the tanner's daughter. These odorous hints were brief but persistent, and made it impossible to ignore the fact that the source of this pervasive pong, this relentless vertical trail of smoke, came from the smouldering flesh and bone of forty-eight bodies.

The smoke itself, it's been said, can still be seen on wind-less afternoons.

Anna veered from the main road to circle round the market square. Scent had once been a map unto itself. Brewer's Lane turned to Baker's Lane and the citrus smell of drying hops had slowly folded under the soft aroma of rising bread, but this was no longer the case. There was no transition in aroma, only the all-enveloping smell of the black smoke.

She wished to merge with the business on the street, to be as unnoticeable as possible. She kept her head tucked downwards, watching her feet poke out, rhythmically lurch-ing and retreating, from under her skirt. She occasionally lifted the basket to inspect its imaginary contents. Her loose curls shook with each stride, cylindrical springs that monopolized her peripheral vision.

Anna could hear the three daughters of Erhard, a harness-maker, and his wife, Rebekka, long before she could see them. They were, as they always were, singing hymns near the church, fresh roses in their hands, tipping their small rounded noses towards the scent they pretended to sell to passers-by:

> *To thee before the close of day,*
> *Creator of the world, we pray*

*That, with thy wonted favour, thou*
*Wouldst be our guard and keeper now.*

*From all ill dreams defend our sight,*
*From fears and terrors of the night;*
*Withhold from us our ghostly foe,*
*That spot of sin we may not know.*

*Holy art thou, our God!*
*Holy art thou, our God!*
*Holy art thou, our God.*

To an outsider, these three girls appeared to be God's devoted disciples, brimming with devotion. They sung not one word wrong, nor wavered in harmony. Their small faces shone with colour from singing so long under the warm sun. The little one, Ursula, named after Rebekka's own aunt, stood in between of her taller sisters, their matching blonde heads glinting under the sun like a church organ's golden flue pipes, freshly polished, ablaze with heavenly auras. They always arranged themselves this way, asymmetrically, like the bottom half of a severed star, as if perched upon a little stage, a choir spreading good cheer.

To someone who had just arrived in town, these were godly children, but the locals who stooped down and dropped a coin in their cup did not rejoice in God's praise, did not linger for a moment to bask in the sweet song of these girls, but rushed past, refusing to take a rose. Not that the girls offered one; they'd given up going so far in their pretence. They no longer bothered to reach up only to yank the stem back as if it were a cherished rag doll. They kept their pert noses firmly stuck to the pink bouquets, the small petals rustling under their singing breath. A look of calm came over their faces with each sniff as if, in that one splendid moment, the euphoric sweetness of the roses concealed all the displeasure they'd ever known up to then.

As Herr Mertzler exited his butcher's shop with slabs of meat to rinse under the fountain, he tried to ignore the rose girls, for this was what they were called now – they were no longer the daughters of Erhard and Rebekka, because neither was alive any more.

Herr Mertzler skirted behind them, feigning to take no notice of anything but the dripping meat in his hands. But the rose girls noticed him; they always noticed, regardless of their apparent inebriation from the saccharine scent of roses. They sung louder, the hymns now a goading chant. Herr Mertzler grudgingly reached for his purse and, without wiping his hands across his red-streaked apron, dropped a bloodied coin in their cup. The girls took another whiff, journeyed to wherever the scent carried them, perhaps to where the line between play and reality could not be blurred so easily, where evil imaginings did not ever spring to life.

It was not too strong a claim to say the children of Flusstal were godless.

# PART I

# CHAPTER 1

*The summer before*

Hans went into the forest to collect kindling. His mood was one of contempt. He begrudged his father's new apprentice, Georg, his spindly and nimble fingers at the weaver's wheel; he was jealous of the way his father hovered nearby praising his work. Hans himself was a clumsy weaver, his fingers were short and wide, fingers he grieved being burdened with each day. So unlike his father's apt hands, so inferior to Georg's gifted hands, his were bungling stubs of bone and tissue. So unfair that these hands should belong to him, so unfair he could not simply cast them off and replace them, or whittle them down with a knife into slender, supple appendages.

After dinner, his father had raised his cup to Georg and told him he had no doubts he would one day be a master weaver, something he had never said to Hans. Though Georg was a year younger than Hans' seventeen, his work was already far beyond anything Hans could accomplish. On this day, the promise Hans always suspected he lacked had been confirmed. He would be nothing more than a fledgling weaver, and Georg would be well-known and sought after for his flawless fabrics.

Hans was sure his father would hire Georg too, the moment he gained journeyman status. Hans' life suddenly stretched before him, a life without distinction; he'd always be eclipsed by Georg. Maybe one day he would not be able to get any work at all, and he would have to go to Georg and ask for employment, who would by then have his own thriving shop, and Georg would hire him out of pity, because of an obligation he still felt towards Hans' father, and Hans would have to work with a pretence of gratefulness. Of servitude.

Georg with his soft curly hair, with his shining front teeth with a space wider than slight between them, who grinned up at Hans when his father sent him to gather kindling, preferring the company of his apprentice to that of his own son. His own son! If a son is ruled by his father, his father only by Jesus and Jesus only by God, then where would such alienation from his father leave Hans but estranged from God?

Later Hans would claim it was exactly this state of mind, one filled with envy, of alienation, especially on the Lord's Day, that left him so vulnerable to the devil's workings.

As Hans scooped up leaves and stray twigs a light rain began to fall. The kindling would be damp by the time he returned home and he would again look less than Georg. He could not even gather kindling with his unwieldy hands before rain soaked it. In a fit of ire Hans dropped the box and kicked it so that all the kindling went flying out. He kicked it several times.

He was further incensed that he had been so stupid as to kick the box so that the dry kindling at the bottom was now wet and muddy and completely useless.

He turned the box over and sat upon it. The rain was becoming heavier and fell against the murky canopy of the forest with an uneven sound like the frenetic fingers drumming against a table. He watched a dark puddle gather near his feet, then looked closely at his fingers, at the cracked skin on his red bulging knuckles, his wide flat fingernails and the heavy padding down each of his thumbs. Squat, he thought, squat fingers. Hans was in no hurry to return to his father's cottage. It was warm despite the rain. He cracked his knuckles, a habit he had begun in hopes of achieving better flexibility through his joints.

'Hans!'

Hans looked round, but couldn't see anyone. The woods seemed to have grown in the waning light, the trees no longer extending upwards but down like dangling ropes hanging from the sky, swaying in the growing wind. It was darker than it should be because of the murky storm clouds and everything seemed to take on the shade of a fresh bruise.

'Hans!'

He stood up, but still could not see who was calling him or if anyone was calling him at all. It happened sometimes at the spinning wheel: he would think someone had said his name but it was only a phantom sound that seemed to erupt from the monotonous sighing and wheezing of the wheel, like an echo of indistinct origin. A sound real enough to make him look up, and yet impossible to have been heard. The puddle at his feet was now a heavy sludge, he tried to lift one of his legs but it seemed too heavy to move. He laughed nervously then, and this surprised him. One never suspects oneself to laugh so oddly when frightened.

'It's me. Georg.' Georg laughed lightly and grabbed Hans' shoulder. Hans startled, his hand jerked upwards and covered Georg's smooth long fingers. 'Your father sent me to look for you.'

'Oh,' said Hans, turning at the waist, for he could not seem to move his feet. They seemed to be pulled into the earth. Georg smiled. His upper lip sprouted a thin line of hair that covered up sparse speckles of white-headed bumps just at one corner of his mouth, or maybe caused them – ingrown hair looping back in and out like stitches.

Georg's hand squeezed Hans' shoulder and pushed him back down onto the box.

'Oh,' Hans said again, laughing, an odd giddy laughter.

Georg knelt in front of him and began to move his hands up his arms, as if trying to warm him. Hans knew what would happen next. It had happened before when he had gone to get kindling. Georg always seemed to follow and the unthinkable ensued there in woods. Afterwards Hans would be unsure what had happened, just as he sometimes believed he heard his name being called as he worked at the spinning wheel, unsure of what he truly heard, the sound possibly only a manifestation of his imagination.

Georg turned him over. Hans' ankles twisted in the mud, his feet never seeming to lift. Georg pulled down Hans' breeches. The rain against his buttocks was a cool crisp sensation that made his exposure even more exhilarating. The air and rain puckered his skin and caused this heightened awareness of his body and all its hidden facets. He felt his body was more than just an impediment to wash and feed; it could also provide something on its own – pleasure – and not only his but someone else's too.

He knew Georg had a part in his body's achievement of such pleasure, but it was ultimately his body's decision to reach such a peak.

Georg pressed one of his nimble fingers inside him. Hans felt an odd pressure that grew into a kind of relenting, an opening up that was not unpleasant, though not pleasant either. It was more the succumbing that Hans felt himself rise to, a giving in. He felt Georg's warm thighs against his, his warm hands on his hips as he positioned himself. Hans lay there waiting, for Georg's thrusting that did not hurt. Keeling over the empty box he rocked back and forth. He watched his hands, his ugly hands, grabbing at tufts of grass and mud, trying to steady himself. He closed his eyes and remembered he had offered to get the kindling – he always offered to collect it – and Georg always followed him out here. They met in the woods, though Hans, in that very moment could not recall when these meetings with Georg had begun. It seemed not to matter. Only that it was happening. Hans could feel Georg, would submit to Georg and his elegant hands. His eyes fluttered open briefly, the ground jiggled, pitched forwards, back; he yielded to the ascending sensation that flowed through him, mounting surrender, he could feel the wet mud squish between his fingers. He would have to pick his fingernails clean with his knife. Remember, he told himself, or his father would be angry that he handled material with dirty hands. Hans looked down as if to impose on his mind an imprint of his muddy hands to better serve his memory later, for this would be the only thing he would allow himself to remember.

He skidded forwards, the kindling box tipped slightly and something stuck into his stomach, a sliver of wood. Georg held on to him harder, his arm wrapped round Hans' neck as if he were a sheep to be sheared.

He could stand it then, in that moment, that he would

never be a master weaver. When Georg was inside him, so was a part of his father's approval; it didn't just belong to Georg then, but spilled off into him.

Hans would only think this later when he tried to rationalize his enchantment. The truth was he thought none of these things with Georg; not of his father, not of his hands, he thought only of Georg's soft dark curls and round eyes, his baritone voice that pulsed up and through his wide hard chest, and that he needed, *needed* to push himself just as Georg pulled him. A release was felt, a release that now it had become known was crucial to their lives.

Georg bit his back, close to his neck as he poured into him with one last shudder. It never took long, maybe that was why he was unsure it happened it all. Georg withdrew from inside him.

They collected the kindling together, picking up leaves and twigs closest to the trunks of trees and between bushes in an effort to seek out the driest, saying nothing. The act they had just committed was now a slow dispersing mist that left no evidence. It was an unspoken agreement that what had happened had not happened, so it could happen again. Denial of this act also meant denial of any feelings of guilt or sense of indecency.

Hans would sometimes experience an obscure disquiet the morning after these interludes with Georg. He would feel cramped being in the same room as his father and Georg, as if there wasn't enough air for each of them. Their movements would occupy his peripheral vision and distract him from his spool. He would feel greatly irritated as if they were in his way, closing in on him, and a kind of disgust would creep over him. He would have to excuse himself to the outhouse, where he would lean his forehead against the wall, the knots in the wood scouring into his brow. He would softly knock his head against the wall and pray, 'Bring me peace, if possible, Lord,' and wait until his breathing slowed and the rage he felt so deeply slowly extracted itself as if it were its own entity that came and went as it pleased, leaving behind little but the hollow where it could again burrow. Once this spell of anger left him, he could not conjure any reason for its presence, any sense of what it felt like, though he had just experienced it moments ago.

When they returned to the cottage Georg remarked to Hans' father that Hans had been sheltering under a tree to wait out the rain, implying that Hans was feeble, even effeminate, for wanting to avoid getting wet. They then began a conversation about weaving and money.

Tomorrow was Monday and Hans was going into Flusstal with his father to contract more work, something he always enjoyed because Georg stayed behind.

Tomorrow Hans would wake in the night when the hail came but draw no connection to the act he committed with Georg to the sudden turn in weather.

# CHAPTER 2

Sitting upright in her bed, her chin resting on her knees, Anna listened to hail fall against the roof in a cacophony of rattling. It had rained yesterday, most of today, and now it was hailing, a great precursor to grief for a tavern-keeper and his wife. It was mid-August; the grapes had just begun to change colour and the vines had been pruned to give the grapes more exposure to the sun, leaving them vulnerable to harsh weather. The storm bells rang out from the tower in the square, a distant ominous throbbing.

She turned and looked down at her husband, but couldn't see his face in the dark. She decided, however, that he wouldn't wake or, better, couldn't. His body twitched slightly as if the hail was penetrating his dreams, and his throat emitted a kind of whimpering moan as he exhaled his snores.

Anna stretched forwards, felt around for the candle on

the table at the end of their bed. It illuminated their small room: the wooden chair beside the table with its worn seat, the pitcher of wine that was never empty or full for long, the small chest against the wall filled with their Sunday clothes and two spare shawls. She was momentarily distracted by the long, strange shadow cast by the crooked column of their four-poster bed; it looked somewhat like a leg that was slightly bent at the knee.

When she turned round again, she was startled to see that Wilhelm's eyes were open and he was looking at her, but his expression was one of confusion, as if he didn't recognize her or know where he was. Did he think he had walked into a guest's room again, and passed out on their floor, or tried to get into a guest's bed, thinking it was his own, that the warm body was Anna's? He blinked repeatedly, trying to locate himself in time and place.

She wasn't sure who she was about to meet: Wilhelm the merry, Wilhelm the fool or Wilhelm the melancholic. Anna had three husbands, really, and they arrived at different but predictable parts of the day and night, starting with the melancholic and ending with the fool. Wilhelm in each and every stage under the drink's influence believed everything he said, believed every side of himself and always spoke with the same earnestness as if he had no idea he would feel different only hours later. The merry man, who people were most familiar with and who did indeed appear for the most hours of a day, was the disposition Anna least liked because being merry was always his objective, the desired end result of his excess, and so she felt most resentful towards this version of her husband.

'What is it?' his words were slurred.

'It's raining.'

He closed his eyes again, and she thought he would simply go back to sleep, but they fluttered open, and he pushed himself up, looking round for the pitcher and child-ishly pointed at it. Anna reluctantly poured him some wine; there was little point in trying to divert him when he was still so drunk, and perhaps it would send him back to sleep.

'It's hailing,' he said, as if correcting her and she knew he was already in his downhearted state and would soon aban-don himself to worry.

The candlelight softened his features, but rather than flattering his appearance, this softening made his eyes and nose seem smaller and, as a result, his face seemed larger, more bloated. Anna could still be startled by how much his intemperance had altered him physically. His cheeks were constantly mottled, a thin sheen of sweat covered his fore-head and there was an overall sponginess to him, as if each muscle in his bulky body had shrunk to make room for more wine.

'It hasn't been going on too long,' Anna said, hopeful that the hail would soon stop and make her statement true.

'But it doesn't take long does it? A minute of hail can ruin a vineyard.' He attempted to emphasize 'ruin', but his voice was too husky to achieve outrage and he broke down into a short coughing fit. He wanted to lure her in, he wanted to be reassured and then say why her assurances were flawed. It was an endless loop that at this moment Anna hadn't the energy to follow, because really, there wasn't anything more she could say that sounded hopeful.

Thrice during their thirteen-year marriage Wilhelm had refrained from excessive drink. The first was when they had just married and perhaps the excitement of a new wife, his new position as husband, had been more alluring than wine, for a short time at least. The second was just after Konrad was born. Wilhelm had stayed relatively sober in the first few months, so pleased was he to have a son. When it seemed that Konrad would indeed live and when Konrad's infancy was in reality less interesting than Wilhelm first assumed, and he realized it would be a long time before his son would be someone he could really make his own, he resumed his old ways. Again he sobered up when Manfred was born, eight years later and after four miscarriages, but this sense of sheepish gratefulness didn't last long either.

In some ways, his drunkenness benefited Anna; she believed it was the reason she did not conceive again, and this for her, was at the time, a small mercy.

She went to the window so she could hear the hail hitting the shutters and attempt to assess its size. She caught a faint reflection of her own face, and it was for a moment unnerving, this combination of hail and seeing a wasted outline of herself.

The hail had suddenly intensified, coming down with greater weight, the sheer volume of the stones hitting the roof was deafening. They both listened in silence with pained alertness, feeling cornered and helpless. Finally Wilhelm began covering his ears intermittently.

'I just can't listen to this, I can't.'

Then he rolled onto his stomach, went up on his knees and turned round in the bed so he could reach to refill his cup with wine but, Anna, foreseeing that he would likely knock the table and spill the pitcher, went and took his cup and by the time she had poured more wine, the hail had stopped.

He leaned back in the bed once she handed him his cup, and as he was about to begin the fretful diatribe that she had predicted, she forestalled him.

'I should see if any of the guests are up.'

This was only partly true. Occasionally a guest sneaked out of their room and fumbled through the tavern or the cellar for a bottle of wine, but her real concern was whether her youngest son had woken.

Anna made her way down the hall towards the room where Manfred and Konrad were sleeping, or at least where she hoped Manfred was still sleeping. She was certain the hail would have woken him, and she wanted to make sure he was still in bed. She moved down the hallway in a state of stifled anxiety, straining to see any faint movements, any undulations in the curtain of darkness just beyond the candle's reach that could be Manfred, jumping up and down to the clamouring hail. That is, if she was lucky enough to find him still inside the tavern.

She hurried down the hall and was filled with an unwarranted confidence that Manfred would be nestled safely in his bed.

Anna noticed there were no slivers of light under the doors, so, it seemed to her, she was the only one wakened by the hail. Maybe it was not so bad then, maybe Manfred had slept through it; she was a light sleeper after all. The inn was at half its occupancy, there were two peasants in one room hoping to sell some pigs, a bookseller passing through and two weavers in from the village. She held the candle up, but suddenly could not remember which door her sons were behind. She stood there frozen, unsure what to do. It was not as if she could go jiggling door handles and waking the guests. The boys slept in a different room from night to night, whichever one was empty, and when none were empty, they slept on the benches below, where Konrad had to watch vigilantly over Manfred, and thwart any attempts at escape outdoors. Anna remembered the first time Manfred did this: she had found him outside, damp and cold, inexplicably standing there as if he had just grown bored with being asleep. Now she understood, well, not understood, but knew it was because Manfred wanted to get something he had suddenly recalled in his sleep that he'd seen earlier, a lost button or a glove on the walkway in front of the tavern, a toad he'd seen in the canal behind the tavern, or leaves, always leaves.

She could hear movement behind one of the doors – a scuffled sleepless pacing – likely the peasants, worried over their livestock and fields. She half expected one of them to crack open the door with an accusatory sneer implying the storm was a surprising fault of the inn like soiled sheets or dirty water, as if the inn was somehow responsible.

The four other doors, in the soft light of the single candle flame, had recently begun to cause a kind of vertigo in Anna as she stepped past them: a sensation of tumbling down, towards nothing in particular but the dark abyss that had yet to be illuminated by the light of the candle and expose the end of the hallway. She worried, that while in the throes of this whirling sensation to steady herself she would grab onto one of the latches and fall through the door and wake up some enraged peasant, who, still under the influence of sleep or nightmare, would come at her with his long, soiled fingernails. Or worse, grab her and drag her into his room. It would not be the first time such a horror happened to a tavern-keeper's wife, and Wilhelm would simply sleep through her cries for help.

So when Anna first heard the scuffled sleepless pacing behind one of the doors, she slowed down, tried to regain her composure, her footing. But her vertigo intensified, from fear she would somehow reach out and lift the latch, an urge that harkened back to those foolish childish impulses to touch that which your mother forbids: fire, a hot pot, a not yet chipped plate, a spider's web still catching flies. She had once suffered, when she first arrived at the inn, urges to swing open the doors to all these rooms to discover various tableaus – of a husband and wife mid-argument, mid-kiss, a peasant in mid-dress, mid-waking, mid-sleep. She wracked her mind for other, more interesting scenes she could come across, but it was impossible for her to think up anything too obscene on her own.

She could hear voices inside the room, but not what they were saying exactly, only that they were having a hard whispered argument and someone was crying, an airy kind of wailing, as if his voice had run out.

It must be the peasants grieving over the weather, but she couldn't remember for sure who had been put in this room. While she reported their guests to the city bailiff, the servant, Margarethe, usually showed them to their room.

Each room held only two occupants, and yet what Anna heard almost sounded as if there were three people inside. She leaned in slightly towards the door, listening. The voices stopped, and silence rose into its sibilant drone. Just as she was about to pull back and continue walking, a noise rang out. She knew it was the chamber pot. The door thumped suddenly as if someone had been thrown up against it. Anna lurched backwards, and hurried down the hall to where she had remembered her sons were sleeping.

She stood a moment, trying to catch her breath and then turned round keeping one hand on the latch. It was quiet again and, as her fear ebbed she became cross, yet again someone had spilled their chamber pot in the dark. Such carelessness was committed often enough by those who thought the tavern was as ephemeral as their stay. It was likely the traveller; it was always those passing through who had little care for the inn they would never see again. They cared nothing for aim, and just as often missed the pot as filled it. Scent was something the innkeeper must always consider. For Anna it was financially impossible to mask the usual pong of an inn with perfumes and rose petals soaking in water, but she felt the need to minimize the odours left behind by so many bodies and so scrubbed the floors once a month, quite well if she did say so herself. She had washed the floors just that morning and felt a familiar swell of frustration of having her labour so quickly ruined. It took quite an effort to subdue the odour of urine. She held the candle up and looked to see if urine was running out under the door and pooling in the hall, but she saw nothing there.

Manfred was awake but still lying down, his blankets were gathered to the right of him, his teeth were chattering. Why he would not cover himself again with the blankets was a mystery to Anna. Konrad slept soundly next to him, rolled up in nearly all the blanket.

She pulled the blanket across Manfred's chest, trying to tuck in his raised arm. He was holding something in his hand, twirling it back and forth. Pulling the blanket out from under Konrad, who burrowed into the bedding as if in a cocoon, roused him awake.

'You shouldn't take all his covers, he'll catch his death.'

'He wasn't using them when I came in from the stable!' Konrad said rubbing his eyes.

Anna attributed the reproach she heard in Konrad's voice lately to having to work in the stables. They had yet to hire another stable boy, the last one having left near a year ago. What could be done? Anna would ask him this in the beginning, 'Do you have an answer? There isn't enough money to feed a stable boy just now. What do you suggest, get rid of you for a stable boy?' Then she would tease him that she and Wilhelm had thought long and hard about trading him in for a stable boy, but decided they were already so used to him it would only be a bother. Or she would say, he could always trade duties with the cellar boy, a much more arduous position, and hoped that Konrad would be grateful they could still afford to keep Caspar.

But such playful teasing no longer cheered him. Anna felt his growing dissatisfaction with their circumstance was now turning into reproach towards her. This caused much argument between them, which ended with Konrad silently threatening to reveal Manfred's condition to Wilhelm by spending the day asking how he could help his father, fetching him wine, laughing exaggeratedly at something Wilhelm said, all the while glancing over at Anna with that menacing look he could give. Anna would feel unable to discipline him. Nonetheless, together they were able to sustain the pretence for now, and Anna hoped it would not be much longer before Manfred would become well again.

The look that passed between her and Konrad was brief, but one that never ceased to make them both feel as if they were about to dissolve under its weight and fragility. In these glances, they never retained eye contact for too long for then the lie could be felt. They colluded in this glance, and colluded to look away at that very moment when the glance seemed to goad them to say it aloud, to say that something was wrong with Manfred.

Anna set the candle down on the small table, but not before giving a quick glance into the chamber pot to see if it needed emptying and it did.

'Did he go in the pot?' she asked Konrad.

'It wasn't me.'

'Oh, that's good. Very good.' She nearly clapped her hands with pride at this small feat by her youngest son. 'Did you see him do it? You didn't need to help him at all?'

Konrad said nothing, but shook his head 'no' as he cupped his hands in front of his mouth and blew into them. It was cold.

27

'Could you go down and put more wood on the fire? And toss the pot, will you?'

Konrad paused, and Anna could feel he was contemplating saying 'no' that he would not, that it was Manfred's piss and so Manfred should do it, but then he quickly flung off the rest of the blanket, picked up the pot and went off downstairs.

'Not too much wood though, it's gone up in price,' she whispered after him.

His small, compact twelve-year-old body slunk off into the darkness. She felt a pull of regret; she put too much on him. Yet this was a fleeting regret, because she always believed she never had to worry about Konrad: he was hard-working and would always do well. His future was neatly plotted before him, and when Anna did feel this sense of guilt for having required his complicity and all that came with it, she would tell herself that Manfred's convalescence was also in Konrad's best interest. It would be Konrad who would one day inherit both the tavern and Manfred if his brother did not become well. She only readied him for the worst possible outcome.

Anna then saw the leaves in Manfred's bed, in the dark they seemed a trail of shelled beetles perfectly lined up, marching forwards in an order of his design. In his hand was his spoon, he was always with a spoon. If Anna tried to pry it away from him, he would rock back and forth waving his empty hand and tears would follow. He would look so incredibly piteous, as if the old rusted spoon was made of gold and the last spoon on earth, or perhaps he believed that without it he would never eat again. Anna was unsure of the significance the spoon held for Manfred, only that she was quite afraid of him in those moments after she took it away. She let him have it most times, and to counter odd looks from guests or tavern customers she would act quite pleased he had it if someone was nearby. 'Yes, that *is* the spoon I wanted. Now hold on to it just for a moment, I don't need it quite now. Keep it till I do.' On the days when she could no longer bear the sight of a spoon in her son's hand, she distracted him in order to take it away without all the fuss. Something else usually made of silver, a candlestick or other items she knew he liked to hoard.

But what was this now, putting leaves in his own bed?

Anna was beginning to find his perplexing collecting more and more disconcerting. And with her feeling jittery, she was startled at the sight of them. There were times Anna felt herself convinced that the infant she had borne had been stolen and replaced with the Manfred she now knew. During these periods of darkness, she felt she should treat him as a changeling, send him down the River Neckar, and see if her true son returned. Her true son would be robust and gurgling, he would look directly at her. But this kind of thinking was reserved for those moments of despair, when Anna asked, 'How could this child be born by me?' She would fall into self-pity: 'What did I do to deserve this?'

But these thoughts quickly turned to steam as the business of the day cooked them away.

'Do you not have enough bedbug bites that you have to bring in leaves to your bed? And what about the other guests, Manfred? Do you think the next man who sleeps in that cot will be pleased to have bits of leaves in his bed?' She whispered this as she brushed the leaves up into her hands and pulled the blankets back up over his slight body. He had not a big appetite, and was small for his four years, not in height, but he seemed to her too slender, too slight in bone. 'Would you drink some milk, if I were to get it?' She did this often, when she could not sleep, try to give Manfred milk. She put aside a small cup of fermented milk to keep in the kitchen. She thought if he fattened, his mind too would become nourished.

He looked up at her and Anna thought that he nodded just ever so slightly in the affirmative. He was slow on his words, and so correspondingly on others' words as well. His quick reaction to her question pleased Anna. 'Milk?' she repeated, though more clearly as if he was a foreigner on the cusp of being able to unfold this alien language, having just spotted a fine tear to writhe through, that single familiar word that could act as that necessary point of reference so the complete question could be understood. From milk, there can be cup, after cup is plate, then fork and spoon all strung together in whole sentences. A complete vocabulary passed through Anna's mind, a future conversation passed between her and Manfred in which they would easily share information about themselves. He could tell her about his collections and they would make perfect sense and he could do more around the tavern and in the stable.

He started to stand up in his bed, his nightgown, much too large, was pulled to one side exposing one of his shoulders and the sharp wing of his collarbone. He was a beautiful child, a diminutive Adonis, his mouth a perfect pink ribbon set in the middle of rounded cheeks, under the bluest eyes, symmetrically aligned in a heart-shaped outline. It was Manfred's eyes that made everyone who noticed him comment on how beautiful a child he was, eyes which seemed to capture and hold light in a way that what was reflected was a luminous world without any hint of shadows. Whoever observed Manfred was momentarily also filled with this lightness, a feeling of renewal, that whatever bother or even hopelessness one felt, it was for a few seconds lifted and replaced with optimism or, at the very least, softened by the presence of innocent beauty.

Manfred's eyes belied nothing of his delay with words, rather they made him seem an especially curious child, so Anna could very easily keep it hidden. If someone were to begin asking Manfred direct questions, she would quickly come along and sweep him away in a show chastisement, 'Oh there you are, you spoiled child, trying to get out of washing the floors are you? Well, you come along with me right now and get on with your tasks.' She would run her hand over his hair to the small of his back, and push him along with her to another part of the tavern all the while smiling warmly at whoever tried to speak to him, so that she was not considered cold or distant. However, for the most part Manfred went unnoticed, because Anna kept him tucked away with her in the kitchen, or beside her when she cleaned the rooms or laundered linens outside. When he was not with her he could usually be left alone for hours and never fuss, completely immersed in his own version of the world around him. People would walk right past him, and if they did eventually notice his presence, say sitting by the kegs, they would only comment, 'What a splendid boy you have there, Wilhelm, if only mine was so well-behaved.'

It was his prettiness that made his silence seem all the more profound, and his beauty all the more intense because of his silence.

But Anna knew this would not last, he would, God granting, become a man one day and his wordlessness would no longer be considered profound.

Up until now, Manfred was subject to monosyllables, 'yes' or 'no' that most often needed to be coaxed from his mouth. Other words were used improperly, or randomly, words he picked up from the tavern without ever grasping their meaning and these he would sing in his lilting chant.

This was how Wilhelm discovered Manfred could repeat many of the simpler tavern songs verbatim, in the exact harmony they were meant to be sung. He could also just as easily sing a hymn, as most were set to the rhythm of much older tavern songs, and he could do this it seemed after only hearing the hymn once or twice. He knew fragments of other songs and hymns, but at last count, he knew six tavern songs and four hymns with perfect accuracy.

This was what changed Anna's mind that her son had gone deaf, something she was convinced of for a short period. What else could explain his muteness and unresponsiveness?

Yes, she had believed this, until she heard him sing.

From time to time, Wilhelm would stand Manfred on a table in the middle of the tavern and begin singing one of the songs until Manfred chimed in and continued through to its end. Anna always took the spoon just as Wilhelm picked Manfred up and he was distracted; he seemed to enjoy that brief moment of weightlessness. This distraction would continue while he sang.

It was meant to be novel, to watch a child so unknowing of the lust and greed, trickery and vengeance he sung about. Much like teaching a foreigner only the pronunciation of profanities in German and watching him ignorantly speak them, to the amusement of one's drinking mates. This was the original intent in having Manfred sing: amusement. However, everyone would go silent as Manfred's light voice spread through the vast drinking room like a dewy mist that tickled the cheeks of listeners, curling round their necks and pulling them in closer.

*There was an old woman who lived under a hill*
*Fa la la, la la la la la la*
*If she's not dead she lives there still.*
*Fa la lo, fa la lo, fa la la la la la la lo*
*A jolly young man came riding by*
*Fa la la, la la la la la la*
*He called for a pot for he was dry.*
*Fa la lo, fa la lo, fa la la la la la la lo*
*He called for a pot, and then another.*
*Fa la la, la la la la la la*
*He kissed the daughter before the mother.*
*Fa la lo, fa la lo, fa la la la la la la lo*
*And when the day was gone and spent*
*Fa la la, la la la la la la*
*He bed the daughter with the mother's consent.*
*Fa la lo, fa la lo, fa la la la la la la lo.*

He always drew the lyrics out, they were not sharp and quick but as if he swathed each in a downy pelt.

Any bawdy song would turn soft on his lips, poetic, from something not quite lustful or vengeful as if his mouth could sift out the baseness in any song, lift lust to love, or covetousness to sympathetic yearning and understanding for the fool.

He could drift mid-lyric, slowing then stopping, his eyes wandering off to the far corner in the back of the tavern, this was when Anna, always close by when Manfred sang, would tap him on his shoulder. Manfred would reprise the song exactly where he left off. This open display always caused Anna great anxiety. What if he did not return to the song, what if he stayed stuck in his drifting stares, what would his audience say then? Would it finally be revealed that his clever repetitions of songs were only that, repetitions?

Laughter and cheer erupted as often as a silent awe when Manfred was finished, though he seemed not to notice. This was taken as humility and made the patrons in the drinking room all the more fond of him.

When Manfred sang a hymn, it was not uncommon to see men break down into tears, feeling their own suffering and the suffering of all men at once. Crying for a lost paradise, when the earth was new, mourning the bitten apple, innocence lost, brought to tears by their exultation of God. Manfred's beauty, with the airy cadence of his voice in combination with the altering virtues of wine, made him seem an ethereal entity, a cherub guarding God's throne. They would also cry out in cheer when the song ended, out of relief, out of sadness, with hope that they would again experience feeling so moved, that there was still respite from drudgery outside a cup.

'That child is too tender for this world.' Anna had heard this claim more than once. She tried not to contemplate Manfred's future, only her short-term vision of hearing him speak at a pace natural to his age. But it was often said to her, usually by men who had drunk too much, after poking her in the side as she stood waiting for her son, that Manfred would be called upon one day to spread the word of God. Word. Their languid eyes filled with bloodshot certainty. As if by saying it, they would make it so. Thus is the deceit of excess wine, it makes one feel taller, stronger, have more presence and in this deceit a man seems to shrink, weaken, become buoyant and unconvincing. Who made such claims, would be disputed much later, as each tried to say they were first in predicting Manfred's fate, when it seemed his fate was good.

Wilhelm would lift Manfred off the table when the song was done and set him on the ground, and begin a toast. 'To a man's sons,' would be his opening. His face filled with an expectation that the adoration received by his son would be equally transferred over to him. Though his own voice, made rasping with drink as it rose in volume, would be such a contrast to Manfred's airy cadence, as if one could hear how life soured in the voice as it lowered and faded with age.

Anna would whisk Manfred away as soon as Wilhelm set him down, give him back his spoon and tell him what a good boy he was for such a lovely song. She would quickly guide him away from the customers. Though again, Manfred seemed neither pleased nor displeased, as if he had already forgotten he had just sung a song. He would easily turn back to his spoon, his collections that were usually stored in odd spots, sometimes outside behind the tavern in the summer, in the corners of the kitchen or wine cellar in the winter, his level of enthrallment never breaking, never even waning. Outside the framework of the song he did not understand what the lyrics meant. He could sing a range of words, but not speak them, words only gained traction in his mouth with melody; it was the sequence, the rhythm he understood, not the words themselves. Anna suspected that Manfred had at some point begun to equate singing with free access to his collections, rocks, leaves, sticks, to his beloved spoon.

Once something was arranged just so to his liking, to what he found rational, he would lie next to it, say to a line of leaves, with his eyes squinting. Studying his arrangement in this fashion, so oddly fixated, if he weren't urged by Anna towards a chamber pot, he relieved himself right there in his breeches and was not even remotely discomfited by it. He would run his spoon alongside the row of leaves, like a general rallying his soldiers or a hunter knocking down wild animals. Anna would sometimes do this; superimpose what she deemed a perfectly normal game a boy of his age would play, over the seeming foolishness of his bland arranging.

Manfred was increasingly becoming a sideshow; there were regular requests to hear him sing. He had yet to reel in new patrons, but still, the regular patrons were requesting him more and more.

Wilhelm was all too happy to seek Manfred out and set

him on the table at a patron's first demand, anything to keep the customers drinking. So he said.

Anna had to find ways to keep him out of view of the patrons. The growing frequency in which Manfred was put on display, in Anna's opinion, made it only a matter of time before he would at some point be exposed. She felt as if his singing was a cloak covering his impediment that was slowly fraying, becoming worn from overuse, and that it would not take long before it had thinned out to nothing.

She was sending him to bed earlier and earlier to avoid Wilhelm. 'He's long asleep,' she would tell him. This only worked part of the time, Wilhelm would just as often pull him from bed as he would not. Manfred, if he was sleeping, would keep his eyes closed all the way down the stairs, and stayed slack against Wilhelm so it was difficult to stand him on the table, causing Wilhelm embarrassment. If he was awake, he would sing.

Anna was surprised at how little of a fuss Manfred made at having to go to bed so early. Now, it made sense, this was how he was spending these extra hours in the room, not sleeping but storing his arrangements next to him. They pervaded even his sleep.

# CHAPTER 3

Anna was filled with such great relief at Manfred's slight nod that she heard herself emit a hiccup of laughter, a gasp of elation. This was the first exchange she had experienced with her son that did not entail pointing to whatever it was she wanted him to respond to, not just once but several times and having finally to lure his eyes by bringing the object she pointed to closer and closer to his face. Mostly she chatted away at him as if he did speak normally; a stream of rhetorical questions. She had planned on getting him milk whatever his response, though she hadn't anticipated one. This was the first time, as far as she knew, that the word milk directly conjured up in Manfred's mind exactly what it should without the presence of actual milk. He knew words, this she was sure of, but not their meaning, as though the words were just hollow.

Those he knew best were yes and no, and Anna felt he

was advancing in their usage. It took less to get him to say yes or no to milk, or bread, or water. 'No milk,' he would answer only once Anna had gained his attention by bringing the milk near his mouth as if to pour it down his throat. He always spoke in a light sing-song voice, his intonation rising at the end as if he were forming a question and not an answer, while also sounding just slightly panicked, unsure of the outcome of what he had just said. Unsure if he would or would not be exempt from drinking the milk.

He preferred no, even at times not meaning it. 'No milk,' he could say and yet reach for it, but Anna would not give it to him until he said yes. It seemed to be working, she thought. She had once pointed at various items, simple things like 'pot', 'cup', 'table'. 'Manfred, look, follow my hands, over there, look now, tree. Say it. Manfred say p-o-t . . . you can say it . . . p-awww-t.' She would elongate the middle, make it sound lyrical, try to push his face so his eyes would see the pot, but it was futile, for no one can puppeteer another's eyes. Her attempt at teaching him would quickly disintegrate into pleading, and then quiet weeping.

So, when Manfred stood up, and stumbled slightly on the hem of his nightgown and Anna caught hold of him, she held him tight to her bosom and prayed thanks to God. She pressed her nose into the crown of his head, breathing in the warmth of the early afternoon, before the clouds set in, and all his newfound potential.

It was when she felt his hand on hers, and then his mouth close down on her shoulder, that she pulled him back and saw anger in his face and she knew he was only after the leaves. He was only after lining up the leaves again.

'No.'

Anna grabbed hold of his fine wrists, and pushed him back down into his bed. Disappointment plunged through her chest, gone was the hopefulness just felt, replaced with the same heaviness, all the more weighty for having experienced a brief cessation.

It's just his humours, they are just imbalanced, it happens, she'd heard that. The humours are off in the early years, they just need to be set like broken bones. That is all. His humours just need to be realigned. This impairment was only a transient state, the way thumb-sucking was for other young children, whatever it was, this offset humour would heal.

Her glimpse of having a speaking son, deepened her yearning that he be cured.

She feared that once it was suspected, it would be too difficult to hide, and the fact of Manfred's speechlessness would spread, and that at best, he would for ever be saddled with the label of idiot. Worse, a singing idiot. It would be not so terrible if his ailment was outward – he might even garner sympathy if it were a lame leg or blindness – but because it was something in his mind he would be considered a senseless being and this would open him up to all sorts of cruelty.

But worst of all there was the economics of feeding a mouth attached to a useless body, no not useless, but indifferent to direction.

'No,' she said again to him, to his condition, as if she could just refuse it, like a slice of bread she didn't want. An image of Manfred locked inside a cupboard, in some travelling Wunderkammer, being gawked at, as he sat and arranged and rearranged leaves, came to her mind. 'The Boy Who Collects and Has Been Collected' or 'The Fixated Boy' would be the silver label above his head. 'Half crow, half boy,' it would read, and there he would be cowering in a corner of his cage with shiny spoons all round him, amid all the other oddities.

The smiling, gurgling infant she had once held, had one day averted his eyes and there they stayed: averted. Anna could feel the foot of time pressing down on her. His four years could barely excuse his remoteness any more; there was much less baby than person in him now. She would not get him any milk.

Konrad slipped back into the room and put the emptied chamber pot down. He stood next to Anna beside the bed, and they both hovered over Manfred as he flapped his hands in frustration and for a moment Manfred seemed their child. Anna pushed this peculiar thought away.

'You shouldn't have let him bring leaves into the bed.'

'I didn't know he had any!' He moved forwards and grabbed Manfred's hands and tried to push them back to his sides.

'Stop it, you'll hurt him.'

'I hate it when he does that.'

'I know. I do too.' Anna sighed. 'Try to sleep. Be sure to share the blanket.'

# CHAPTER 4

Ten bells always arrived too early in a tavern the night before, but in the morning, last call had not come early enough. Anna likened the tavern in the first morning hour to an animal slowly rising. The floorboards creaked like stiff joints snapping into place, the wood-panelled walls groaned as they gained heat. The odd coughs and yawns and tinkling in chamber pots, the hushed whispers between room-mates who were long acquainted, and the tense noises of those who had never seen one another until the previous night, was its slow rousing, an animal that would shake off the clinging pellets of slumber and eject the guests. Though never before breakfast was served.

The Myrrh Tree tavern had once been a reputable establishment, with an envious location along the main road close to the entrance to Flusstal so that it was the first upright place a tired and thirsty traveller would come upon.

There were a spattering of other taverns upon first entering the city but these were only backstreet wine sellers or small, cold drinking rooms, with only hard benches to sleep upon, making Wilhelm's wine tavern appear even more stately, the mirage that rises from days in a desert come true. It was further out from the wine market, where the finer taverns reigned with their ornate signs, inviting opulence and fine wines, and so it rested on the threshold between the lesser and better of taverns.

Not that the Myrrh Tree tavern's reputation was yet in dispute, but it was on the decline and was considered by most locals a fledgling inn and tavern with low-grade wine.

The height of the tavern's eminence came before the Thirty Years War. Wilhelm's grandfather had wanted to turn it exclusively into a merchant's rest stop, investing to give the tavern an ornate appearance. But he underestimated the cost, the merchant's ability to see through cheap copper and even cheaper hanging tapestries.

Wilhelm's father once longed to make the tavern a regular meeting place of the guilds, putting up a wall to make a separate room off the drinking room, quite perfect for the guilds to manage their affairs, initiate new journeymen, discuss new contracts. But the war reached Flusstal, the plague followed, and the room saw more billeted soldiers than guildsmen. Soldiers who drank and ate, then reneged on the bill. When the war ended, the population of Flusstal had been reduced by half, resulting first in less customers, and also in guildsmen becoming increasingly exclusive about who they let into their guilds while their stunted growth made finding places to meet or taverns to frequent unnecessary.

So neither Wilhelm's grandfather nor his father secured their goal, abandoning their visions of owning a better tavern and bobbing thereafter on the tide of disappointment and wine that followed. Wilhelm's grandmother and mother, tottered along next to them.

Wilhelm too found a wife who had the same patient qualities. Though he had no such lofty hopes for the tavern, he followed in his father's and grandfather's footsteps in breaking the golden rule that a tavern-keeper should always be a purveyor of wine before he is a consumer of it.

But though the ivy that grew up the front of the tavern had in very recent years become too thick, and the stone front become too mossy and there were two shattered panes of glass in the front window, and the door hung just slightly askew, there was still much left of the elegance of Wilhelm's grandfather. The elegance had faded, that was true, and did require one to look for it, but once the copper mountings were illuminated in just the right light from the fireplace, there it was.

Anna liked to seem to make a fuss in the mornings. She would take on a cheery cadence to her voice, one filled with what she believed sounded hospitable and did not show any of the strain that went into the bowls of food she would set before the guests. Meals, the preparation and planning of, the careful consideration of the cost of turnip, of fruit, of meat, salted herrings and bread, the careful negotiation between providing filling meals that would leave the guests satisfied, as well as being financially sensible, were a difficult task.

Anna scooped the boiled oats from the pot and into the bowls Margarethe held out on a tray; a thick gruel that could just as well suffocate a guest, as feed him. A better tavern would serve it with some sausage and light-coloured rye bread. But here the oats were served with dark chestnut bread to scoop it up. Anna sliced the bread thick, and gave less gruel; the bread was cheaper.

Margarethe gripped the tray tightly, her knuckles like white suns against a chapped red sky. She had yet to retreat into full acceptance of remaining unmarried. The tray she held was her opportunity, always, to be noticed as she bent forwards and placed the bowls of food in front of the guests. She muttered all the time, little announcements, a steady narrative of all her tasks, 'Get this bread in now . . . Have to get some water . . . Better add another carrot.' Margarethe the mutterer. Moon-faced Margarethe.

A very specific kind of woman is sent from the country into the city to earn her dowry in a tavern: ones with flat noses, protruding ears, severe overbites. Ugly women, whose prudent fathers know that their odds of securing marriage for their daughters were best in a tavern, where ugliness softens under the low glow of the fireplace and the misty haze of wine.

But she could not muster lightness, or feign enthusiasm that would have bettered her chances to seem appealing in the atmosphere of a tavern. Ironically her focus on marriage made her seem monotonous and dispirited, even grim. She exuded nothing enticing but already appeared the severe wife that often drove men to the wine tavern in the first place. Nevertheless, she was a good servant and likely, in all her gratefulness, would never have uttered a single sharp word towards her husband if she were ever to have one, and Anna hoped she would.

There was a point of controversy between her and Anna. Margarethe often brought Wilhelm his bottles of wine or another measure of brandy in the morning, whereas Anna felt if he were forced to come down and retrieve the wine, he would be forced to dress himself and at least be up and about. Anna was convinced that getting Wilhelm out of his room was imperative in slowing his fall into drunkenness too early in the day. Even now, he was still in his room, in his chair, at his table, bent over the ledgers. It was all an act, he stayed there until he had enough brandy to feel perked up, to banish the brewing illness in his gut and the pounding in his head.

Once Anna would have asked Margarethe to make herself scarce in the mornings, not to go up to Wilhelm's room and ask if he was in want of anything. Both she and Anna knew he would want only wine. Anna would have asked her to clean the linens, make purchases at the market, anything to be outside the tavern and not within beckoning distance. But Margarethe never conceded to this, she was not a servant who conspired with the mistress of the household as some do for the wife to gain their warmth.

Instead she avoided Anna when she took the wine to Wilhelm, and if Anna tried to intercede, she quickly asserted, 'I cannot defy the head of the household, Frau Wirth.' She would pass Anna, shaking her head 'no' all the way up the stairs. There was nothing Anna could do; Margarethe was right, a servant had much better align herself with the master of the house, regardless of how miserable the mistress could make her life. In the end, if Anna wanted to send Margarethe off, Wilhelm would disagree and she would stay. Not that Anna ever mistreated Margarethe for slighting her requests, she knew Manfred made her vulnerable to the hearsay spread by servants. It would only take Margarethe a few sentences to other servants for the secret of Manfred's oddness to be made known. If they were all in the kitchen and Anna asked something particularly demanding of her, Margarethe would take a long glance at Manfred and Anna knew it was a threat.

Thus, they were stalemated, and had long ago put away their arsenal to wage their subtle battles. As it was,

Anna had never heard a single word against Manfred, and so had mostly convinced herself that because Margarethe was completely preoccupied with securing marriage, she was ignorant of Manfred's speechlessness. She believed Margarethe's thoughts and conversations with other servants were only about prospective husbands and perhaps a sharing of knowledge that eased their servile duties.

This made Margarethe tolerable. For the most part they left each other alone.

Manfred sat quietly on the floor beside the table meticulously pulling the stalks from turnips. The spoon had been abandoned by his knee, but not out of his reach. He found a yellow turnip flower in the leaves, and he was going over each of four turnips very slowly in hopes of finding another one.

If it were not for the small scratches on her knuckles he had made when he tried to pry open her hand, Anna would have forgotten the apprehension he provoked in her the previous night.

She heard the scraping of the tavern door and peeked round the kitchen doorway. She could feel Margarethe standing so close behind her that her breath stirred the hair that strayed from her coif and tickled the nape of her neck. This annoyed Anna.

'Take these out first. I think one of them might have left.'

'The weaver's son,' Margarethe answered.

She always knew the guests by face and not number. She could always identify exactly who it was that suddenly departed in the early hours before his breakfast while Anna more often realized this fact by way of being a number short from the night before. She would have to recall the list she or Wilhelm had reported to the city bailiff and deduce from there who was missing. She was glad that Margarethe had this talent for remembering faces, even if it was because she searched the faces of all the guests in the hope one would be her future husband.

Anna removed a bowl from the tray as Margarethe steered towards the guests, and was about to spoon the oats back into the pot to keep warm over the fire, when the doors scraped again. The weaver's son had returned.

Anna was insistent that guests eat their morning meal, even if it were better for her if they didn't as it was included in the fee for their stay and there would be more left over to serve the next morning. All other meals had to be purchased separately, so she could never appear less than adamant that the morning meal be eaten. It wasn't very often the meal was turned down, but even for those who had indulged too heavily in drink the previous night and their stomach was nothing but a catapult or funnel, she still had to appear adamant. Arguing with guests to take even just a spoonful or two was, after all, good hospitality. If their wife stayed as well, Anna would say nothing, but leave the bowl on the table for the wife to have extra.

Anna tried to make herself agreeable to the wives when-ever she could. She knew a tavern-keeper's wife represented the mistress that the tavern itself was – where their husbands spent their money, would rather spend their time, where their hearts hovered so attentively over their cups. Towards the men she acted as wife or mother to distance herself from the centuries old image of the tavern-keeper's wife as procuress. Anna was always mind-ful of such notions and did what she could to undermine them.

Morning in the tavern was nothing like it was at night as there was always a kind of sombreness in the air; of morn-ing regrets, confusion or irritability, reluctance or nervousness to begin daily business. Usually too much had been lost at dice or cards, and the morning exchanged courage for recklessness.

This morning, it was the hail, rather than the wine con-sumed the previous night, that led to the sombre mood. Anna assumed the weaver's son had gone out to see the damage caused by the hail storm.

'How is it out there?' she asked as she placed the bowl in front of him.

She tried to sound optimistic, but wasn't at all certain if the damage from the hail was significant, so her voice sounded too excited, too nervous and then, to cover for this, she let out a light hum that she was immediately embarrassed about.

She had sent Konrad out after they had their breakfast. However, it was still so early in the morning, and she wasn't sure how much he could find out about the state of the vineyards. A panic welled up in Anna. Hunger was always a single tempest away; the Riders of the Apocalypse had been through here before. Anna could recall hunger, deep, bitter hunger, because she had been born in 1633, in the middle of the war. There was hunger of the stomach, hunger not for peace, as that had by then turned into an obscure and distant notion but for stillness, hunger for health, for sleep, for skies not blackened with smoke. Hunger that greyed the faces of everyone and was as innate a feature as the eye colour, the slope of one's nose, the shape of one's mouth.

But the weaver's son said nothing, and a grave silence ensued.

The question on the weather died, unanswered. The weaver's son seemed not to notice Anna or her enquiry. Anna could feel herself flush a faint red for having been so blatantly ignored. It was his father, whom he sat beside who answered, 'God's fury is upon us.' He whispered it, not in fear, but as a fact he had come to accept, that had overcome some previous understanding.

His son's head was pitched forward so the knots in his neck poked out through his parted hair that cascaded down his shoulders. When his father spoke he looked up, though not at anything in particular.

53

Anna saw his lip was swollen, there was a lump on his cheek under his left eye and above his eyebrow was an open cut just beginning to scab over. Before reaching for the spoon sticking out from the oats, he wiped the cut with the back of his hand so that a streak of brownish blood ran across his hand. She recognized him now, last night when they arrived for the evening meal they took a pitcher to their room, instead of staying in the tavern, saying they needed a good night's rest for they had many affairs to tend to the following day. But now as they sat there, they seemed in no hurry at all.

After they finished eating, and all the other men had left the table and gone on with their business, the weaver and his son remained at the empty table as if unable to get up.

# CHAPTER 5

Konrad planned to run all the way to the wine market. He pretended to be a mercenary coming into this newly conquered land for the first time.

The city did appear conquered. Some barrels were on their sides, the gutters had overflowed and there was an all-around stench of refuse and rot. Konrad tried his best to leap over the puddles, but sometimes his foot sank into the pulpy mess.

Konrad liked to run, he believed the breeze he felt as he sprinted would lift the scent of manure from the stables off his skin. But today, there was no escaping the stink of sewage. The air was heavy and humid, a kind of suspended invisible paste, a grey-blue mist. Everything was slightly bloated and spilling out from its edges – vaporous, filmy.

To pretend to be a mercenary was a game he and the cellar boy played whenever they had a chance, usually in the hour before the midday meal, before the tavern became too busy. They would impale one another with fake arrows, make the sound of canons with their mouths; they killed one another over and over.

Konrad hosted fantasies of becoming a mercenary when he was old enough to join an army; he yearned for a life of adventure. It was not as if he didn't want to inherit the tavern, and even during fits of anger when he swore to himself he would leave as soon as he could, he could sense the falsity of this statement. But, although he yearned for adventure, he wasn't a particularly adventurous child. He disliked the cellar because it was so dark and cramped. He was the last to jump from the pier into the river, but mostly he avoided it altogether, and he never ventured outside the routes he was most familiar with when sent out on a task such as this.

Mercenary recruiting stations for far-off wars were set up in taverns, offering a free measure of wine and a gulden for anyone who signed up. The recruiting officers always began their presentations to the customers with stories of famous mercenaries who had retired and now lived in fine houses, wore fine clothes, ate fine food served by fine slaves. They had set up a number of times in Konrad's parents' tavern, because the more financially desperate drank their wine there. A man under the influence was their easiest recruit, especially one who craved another cup of wine so badly and was given the money for many more cups of wine, enough to forget what he had signed up for, at least until morning. Some recruits would try to renege the following day, but they usually could not return their first payment, so would have to go or be arrested for theft.

The tales of great mercenaries deeply appealed to Konrad and Casper, for they were under the influence not of wine but of the childish misconception of one's own abilities. Though Konrad doubted Caspar's ability to succeed as a soldier, he was certain of his own future success and spent much time daydreaming of his coming wealth and fame. It gave him something on which to base his suspicions about himself: that he was indeed extraordinary. He sometimes even looked down at his hands and considered all their future possibilities: the weapons they would one day wield, the women they would touch, the foreign grasses they would run over in strange foreign places, the hair that would one day sprout from below his knuckles and the rough blistered look of his palms. Again and again he pictured his homecoming after a long absence. His mother would run out of the tavern and fling her arms round his neck.

Everything, of course, would have fallen apart in his absence, and this would be when he would finally take over the tavern. His father and Manfred were peripheral characters in this future, but his mother was constantly there, admiring him for his cleverness and the stories he would tell about his time as a soldier.

It was not as if Konrad and his mother had shared any unusual affection for one another prior to Manfred's birth. But since Manfred went sour they had a special bond in their collusion to keep it hidden, first from his father and then from everyone else. But as Manfred grew and his obsessions with his stupid leaves and such intensified, he was becoming more difficult to contain and make excuses for. Konrad had lately begun to feel that his mother had unjustly forced him into this collusion, into watching over Manfred as if he were a daughter instead of a son. She was always pushing him to keep Manfred with him in the stable and teach him this or that: greetings, farewells, the words for straw, bale, horse, cow, saddle. It went on and on.

He was in a constant state of irritation over his brother's apparent speechlessness, for it reflected on his own inability to teach him words and, as a result, what he imagined to be his mother's growing disappointment in him.

For the longest time Konrad had so firmly believed in his part in this deception, that he had been filled with self-importance at the tasks Anna set for him: 'Keep an eye on Manfred', 'Keep him out of the way', 'Make sure he doesn't get out of bed'. He had done all these things with a sense that he was securing the greater good by keeping the truth about Manfred from his father, helping to secure his mother's illusion that Manfred was not yet fine but soon would be. He was so attuned to all the ways his mother subsisted on Manfred's impending wellness that he felt utterly responsible for any fissure in the facade, even for Manfred's apparent inability to get better.

Having all this to defend, the utter weight of it, had made him exaggeratedly defensive. So much so that it took very little for him to feel as if he were being blamed somehow for something, anything, and he felt the nuances of blame crowd in on him with each of his mother's sighs. And if her requests for him to carry out some task were not posited just so, without any insinuating intonations, he could feel himself become angry. His mouth moved before he had time to prevent it, words spilled out before he had any idea of what he was saying. And then, just moments later, Konrad would want to win her back, he would say or do something that released the tension between him and his mother, but his mother would not let him back in, not until she needed him to do something for Manfred.

Konrad used to like the jokes about trading him for a stable boy, the way his mother tugged his ear afterwards, drawing out a smile from his pout. To him it meant she needed his forgiveness in some small way and this meant she loved him. But lately, she said nothing, only shook her head or sighed with disappointment, as if it was all too much that Konrad would want that tug on his ear, the light-hearted jest. Immediately, out of rejection, he would say something back, some kind of retort that invoked her anger, for example that the tavern looked empty again.

It was only in the last year that he had become so sick of

all the deceit. Not the deceit that he had to partake in on the part of his mother, or even his mother's self-deception, for in truth he always closely followed the path that would please her most in the end. It was Manfred's deceit.

Konrad truly believed Manfred was faking. If he could sing on and on in the tavern, then he could surely speak: he just didn't want to. He just wanted to get out of doing chores; it was just a big elaborate trick to keep their mother closest to him. How she had marvelled last night over him pissing in a pot by himself! Whereas Konrad knew all along Manfred could always go in the pot, only he chose not to at times out of simple laziness, or because he couldn't always tear himself away from whatever he was doing, or maybe even just to watch his mother or brother clean up after him. Oh, his singing – how it grated on Konrad. He had had enough of his sickening singing. In fact, he was glad to be in the stable most of the time to get away from it. The way everyone extolled his voice (which Konrad didn't think was all that great anyway), the way his mother's face turned pink with pleasure, as if nothing else in the world mattered, as if no other possibility of such contentment could ever exist. And the more Manfred sang, the more his mother pushed Konrad to join her in instructing Manfred.

And all the while, Konrad knew – he could see it in his brother's face – that he was lying.

This suspicion had been confirmed on more than one

occasion, when he was trying to get Manfred to say something and Manfred would break out into this spontaneous laughter, as if he just couldn't take another minute of it. Konrad knew he was laughing at him, and getting away with it.

Konrad slowed from his sprint. Why was he rushing? It was nice to be out of the stables, and the hail damage, however bad, could not be changed now.

He was stricken by the eerie sight of the nearly abandoned market. It seemed impossible that in just an hour, there would be the usual rush of local tavern keepers and merchants, buying wine to take up the River Neckar and sell elsewhere for more, carters manoeuvring round stalls and vendors selling herbs and salt, fish and livestock, crowds of peasants selling their willow baskets and jumble of other wares.

The tax office, where the wine was measured, marked with a seal and the tax paid, was not yet open, but lamps burned brightly inside. There were also lights in the windows of the Council House. A light drizzle had begun to fall. Would it be the afterbirth of the storm from the night before, mere shudders, or the beginning of another downpour?

A prisoner in the stocks was moaning in front of the Council House, obviously left out all night, his bare feet red from lashings and maybe the hail. There was a sign beside him. Konrad went up to look. It showed the man selling underweight bread. In one hand he took money from a woman, in the other he had the heel of a loaf hidden behind his back. He wore a long cape, which baker's never wore inside their shops. His face was long and wicked-looking, his eyes dark and his nose jutted out into a narrowed point. When Konrad stepped back the man looked very different; there was nothing wicked-looking about him there in the stocks. So then, he'd been cured of his wickedness.

'Best to sell bread for the right price.' Konrad said to him. He circled round once, amused, still thinking of himself as a mercenary, this man his prisoner.

The man said nothing.

Konrad bent down, leaned in close to the man's ear, 'Best to sell bread for the right price,' he said again. He wanted a reaction, for the man to thrash about. Perhaps he would have gone on. It was one's civic duty to humiliate the criminal after all, and since no one was around he could relish this feeling of superiority, but he was distracted by the sight of a carter just a short distance away and he galloped off.

# CHAPTER 6

Anna busied herself while she awaited any early news from Konrad. She placed small bowls of water in the rooms so the guests could wash their faces at the end of their day if they so choose. She went about making the beds and sweeping the canopies suspended over them clean of any vermin that may have dropped from the ceiling, stepping on those still alive, and scooping them up into the ash bucket. She shovelled ash from the fireplaces and emptied the wooden flea traps. In a better inn the flea traps would be made of ivory. She changed the candle in the small awning over the trap, scraped out the water and sap filled with little black specks and filled up the tray again. She marvelled at how many fleas were kept out of the beds, tricked by the heat of a candle to believe they were being led to a warm-blooded body to nip and drink from and, further, how fleas must witness other fleas squirm to their deaths in the sap

63

and yet still go towards it. She swept the corners clean of vermin, then shook the curtains hanging round the beds free of ashy residue and moths.

In the beginning Anna had felt a small thrill while in the rooms when the guests were gone for the day, as if glimpsing into the intimate lives of others. Here was where they undressed and slept and, if with their wives, may have left evidence of libidinous acts. And later when they returned and Anna served them their supper, she would continue to feel hints of this same titillation because they remained unaware of the personal knowledge she had of them.

From the very beginning, Anna was intrigued by the tavern if not so much by Wilhelm. He did hold a certain fascination, but this was entirely linked to the tavern. He had something others wanted – wine and a place to drink it – and this bestowed on him, on all tavern-keepers regardless of their tavern's status, a kind of popularity or, at the very least, notoriety that other men do not enjoy.

If she had to spend the rest of her days beside her husband at his worktable, let it not be a shoemaker with the unyielding aroma of leather, or a cobbler with the stench of long, worn boots too old to properly mend. Let it not be a ropemaker with his chafed hands, or a butcher with blood constantly dried up under his fingernails, let it not be an apothecary with all his strange elixirs and ailing patients knocking at their door. Let it not be a clockmaker like her father.

When she was still under her father's roof, she often passed a tavern close by. The loud, rowdy singing and the laughter could be clearly heard in the street. A liveliness so opposite to her father's whirring, ticking clock shop, so devoid of the silent measuring of time passing, the holding of breath while positioning the verge escapements that needed to be placed just so, so the crown wheel could act like a net to capture and quantify odourless, soundless, tasteless time. Let it not be another lifetime of dull sifting through the entrails of clocks.

Anna never regretted marrying Wilhelm, even after the slow discovery that her husband was a drunk. She loved him regardless. It was as involuntary as blinking. She loved him as she did the tavern, perhaps because of it; she made no separation between the two. Anna had ever entertained any different thoughts about him; it simply never occurred to her not to love him. At worst, they fell into despondent silences with one another, but the business of running the tavern made this impossible to indulge in for long.

She wished her husband didn't make himself ill and foolish; she wished he took more care of the accounts and aspired to be better; that he didn't drink so much it put them near debt. Her love was frustrated, but never had she wished for a different husband.

Anna suggested the orders to Wilhelm, who wrote them down; she went to the market more often than him to place the orders and search for good prices and she did the haggling. The responsibility of keeping them ahead of the jaws of debt was Anna's. Like most families, their lives intersected at the evening meal, in bed, on the way to and from church, during their short exchanges on business, until the years stretched from one to the next, netting their fair share of happiness and sadness. There was nothing unusual about their marriage.

She closed the curtain round the bed. The drawn curtain was a result of Wilhelm's father's good thinking. Like wigs and fashion, privacy was no longer solely an extravagance of the elite, cheaper versions were available for those of lesser means.

Privacy was a commodity that the inn traded in. At least it offered the perception of privacy. The doors did not have locks – this was forbidden by the city council because only adulterers would want them, but the curtain round the bed gave guests a sense of being a master, with his own bed-room. This was only true, of course, when the inn was not at full capacity and a guest was forced to sleep with another guest. Still, it was a luxury that kept the inn from sinking to a lesser status. It appealed to those of better means and drew in those with just enough.

It was not that one did not expect a tavern-keeper's wife or servant to enter a room and change the flea traps or replace a candle if need be. Some did not even empty their own chamber pots in the privy beside the stable. It was that she was supposed to uphold some sort of invisibility in the process, invade the room when it was empty. All in the name of privacy.

She knew she was in the weaver's room because there was an order sheet left behind on the small table between the two beds. She noticed the chamber pot had indeed been tipped over and had rolled across the room. The corner of the sheet on one of the beds, where the son must have slept, had streaks and blots of blood. Oh, how much effort this would take to remove, Anna thought. She would have to submerge the linen in milk to bleach out the blood, but never do such stains come out completely. Some slight outline was always left, crusted lilypads of another's secretions.

This was something Anna had not been prepared for when she first married Wilhelm: the excrements of guests. Blood, snot wiped against the side of the bed or under it, fingernails bitten off and spat on the floor, shedding themselves, as if to do so was like a trail of breadcrumbs to help them find their way back.

The chamber pot had thankfully been empty.

What an odd couple, the weaver and his son. The father had unexpectedly decided to leave after breakfast. He went up to the room without his son and retrieved a small burlap sack filled with their belongings. His son remained on the bench even after his father mumbled to him to get up. The weaver waited patiently for a moment or two, then leaned down and began whispering in his son's ear.

He had a long, concave face with a slightly jutting chin that from the side, seemed much like a half moon, the kind of man one easily recognized due to the originality of his features. His son did not resemble him much, except for the strong chin, because his features were spread further apart. You could draw the relation between the two only if you envisioned the father's face as ironed out or the son's to be more compact.

Anna could not hear what it was he said, but there seemed to her, a kind of wheedling in the weaver's hand motions, quick cuts made by upturned hands. His son turned red as if about to weep, and then slowly the colour drained from his face. He finally nodded at his father's demands, stood, muttered 'Yes', as he went towards the door behind his father. 'Yes' he said again before stepping out from the tavern, pausing at the threshold, as if in an argument with his body. The rising daylight scarcely entered through the door, but it carried with it the smell of rain.

She picked up the basin of wine, left in their room the night before on their arrival. It was untouched. She picked out the small insects floating in it, bobbing on the surface like miniscule capsized boats and set it down by the door, so she could pour it back into one of the bottles. This was not a time to be wasteful.

Manfred went with her from room to room. She tried to put it off as long as possible, but when he became restless

Anna would give him something she knew he would be occupied by – some twigs, pebbles, leaves. Today she allowed him to keep the turnip flower. This was better than him glaring into that spoon of his. Giving Manfred items he could fix on was something she felt conflicted over, but he would never stay sitting still for long with nothing in front of him. If he roamed through the tavern looking for things to collect she had no control over who would see him.

Her protection of Manfred was, in a way, due to self-preservation. For if her son's ailment was known, Anna would also be looked upon suspiciously. 'What went wrong there, in that woman's cavity?' people would ask. She would move round the tavern like a pariah – the woman who must have laughed too much while carrying Manfred, who likely felt envy towards a neighbour, or was too lazy while in labour and had not pushed hard enough when her infant son was rested there on the cusp of life, drowning in the filth of her womb.

Once such a status came down upon her, she would have to pursue her defence, she would have to blame the mid-wife, or the lying-in maid for having done something to Manfred, for having envied her fertility and spoiling her son by trying to feed him with old withered breasts. She would have to make a strong case as to why it took a year and a half later for their spells to work. She might very well have to make an accusation of witchcraft.

She would have to blame Wilhelm, reveal to the world

that it was his tainted seed, that it was he who brought down God's wrath on them both, and their son, for his drunkenness.

Who would want her then? She would be cast as a betrayer of husband and household.

In the end, she would still have this son who she had given birth to. That wouldn't change.

She turned and looked at Manfred. His small hands twirled the flower back and forth. He looked happy, no not happy, but content – happy was too strong an emotion for him. It was rare, but sometimes he cried. She would hear him, turn round, and there he would be sitting cross-legged, his small knees exposed like two sculpted stones, weeping. His nose might be stuffed or his head warm, but at other times she could not at all understand why he was crying. Perhaps it was that he was beginning to feel the weight of the unspoken bottled up in his throat, and it came out in fits and sputters. He would not let Anna hold him, but writhed out of her embrace. The only time he touched her was to lightly tap her cheeks with his spoon. If she sat down across from him, he would pick up his spoon and put one small warm dimpled hand on one cheek, then pat the bowl of the spoon against her other cheek. His breath, not yet turned bitter, smelt really of nothing at all, as if he'd barely begun.

She wasn't sure why he did it, but she liked the feel of his touch on her face; it tickled. Anna only let him do it sometimes, it wasn't something she should allow, but the coolness of the spoon and his deep breathing brought on a drowsiness which made her momentarily complacent. Perhaps she also let him do it when she felt in need of affection, and perhaps, she reasoned, he could be coming round. The spoon may be in his mind a drumming stick and at other times a sword. Do children not make toys out of the oddest things? Anna would mourn missing that period of being so loved, of being an admired and intriguing curiosity that solved all sorrow and maintained all happiness. This was the secret gift of motherhood, Anna thought, that had bypassed her with Manfred – those few years when one is so unconditionally loved, so unwaveringly considered capable of anything, everything.

It had been so much easier with Konrad. Once he had learned to speak he wouldn't stop. He pointed at everything round him and said it out loud, then always looked to her afterwards for agreement as if the world existed only on her approval. When she held him on her lap, he would sink into her and if she let him he would stay there for hours examining her hands, asking why to everything she said. She basked in the rush of love that passed between them.

'If something is too close to your eyes, you can't see it properly.' Anna bent down and gently pulled Manfred's hand, which held the small flower, away and held it. He stared firmly at it. She knew once she let his hand go, he would again draw the flower back. Once he had found a shard of glass and held it so close to his eyes to gaze at that he cut himself just under the bottom lid on his left eye. The cut healed and by God's grace had left no scar. Oh, how tragic it would have been for his lovely face to be marred. What would he have been left with then? For the time being, she corrected herself, before he was healed. She said a prayer, the same prayer always.

*Gracious Mother of Jesus, God intends my son's body to be a temple of the Holy Spirit. May it be by your gracious intercession that my son receives God's healing power, so that he may seek him, serve him, enjoy him and depend on him, through the physical life he has given him and shared with him, in Jesus Christ my Lord. Amen.*

She forced his hand to make the sign of the cross against his chest – the coordinates of God.

When she released his hand, he pulled the flower against his face. She sighed, more frustrated than usual. Then she prayed that the hail damage be minimal.

'Frau Stauder is here.' Margarethe was at the door.

Where was Konrad, she thought, he should be back by now. Anna doubted Elsie would have any news on the hail and had no interest in gossip; she was annoyed at Margarethe for saying she was available.

72

She noticed then that Margarethe had a tray with yet another brandy to take to Wilhelm.

'I'll be just a moment, wait here,' she said to Manfred who was still sitting, eyes half closed as he ran the turnip flower up and down his cheeks.

# CHAPTER 7

Manfred saw the world in its detail rather than in its entirety. He moved through his day in constant awe of what others could not see, for their eyes were not attuned to the same intricacies that bombarded his own vision.

It was light that Manfred was engrossed by: the endless refraction of the sun's rays, the way light thickened or lightened the various colours. On a sunny day, a green leaf plucked from an oak tree would appear slick and waxy, but on a cloudy day this same leaf would appear much more verdant without the polish of the sun. The leaf itself was self-contained, was its own metamorphic world. Its yellowy veins set like a meandering river between banks of frothy green meadows that cared little of its origin, showed no sign of strain while being plucked, no shudder at its certain demise, but the eventual desiccating change from green to glorious yellow as if the veiny river ruptured, and finally a brown filled with all the confidence of death.

Not that Manfred had any fascination with death, he thought only in images, brightly coloured images. So, for him, a browned leaf was equal to the word *death* and this is how he understood it: a brown leaf curling up at the edges, retreating back into the ground or being swept away by the wind. Hardly worth mourning, a leaf. A leaf of a rich earthly tone, matching up so perfectly to the soil it would be mashed into. There were so many leaves; one replaced another, hardly worth mourning, a leaf.

He held no sense of singularity, only again, that before death, before a leaf dried and crumbled so easily in his hand, it turned a brown colour, that was beautiful in spite of all its plainness or because of it.

That a colour, however unique, could be found again elsewhere.

Matching up colours was an urge Manfred experienced rather then consciously considered. He collected a wide variety of hues, leaves that could be ordered by colour so that shades of green and brown acted as bookends and all those in between provided a breathtaking spectrum. He spent hours in and behind the tavern seeking what he needed.

He yearned for a kind of orderliness of colour and making piles of say, all brown or green or yellow, inspired calmness inside him. If he had had access to all the colours in the world, he would have carefully arranged them according to shade, so he could become fully immersed in each colour at will. When he wanted red, a colour he encountered mostly in ripened apples, wine, honeysuckle berries, which evoked a gleefulness, he could go there and *be* with red. Perhaps this wasn't exactly the reason for his drive behind arranging colours, one can only surmise, perhaps it was just that the setting out on a task to accomplish orderliness was cathartic in its purposefulness. To stake out small claims of orderliness amid the grand disorganization of the world may have been enough. Once he made his separate piles he would just as soon move on to something else, or mix the colours only to put them back in their order. The repetition of this task must have offered Manfred some kind of happiness, and perhaps it was the rapture he fell under while carrying out his mission, rather than the task itself, that drove him.

But more than colour, it was light that enticed Manfred, or better, the combination of light and colour. Most astonishing to him, was that which reflected light: glass, quartz, mirrors, the river's surface, his spoon. Prisms that held still the commotion of light. In his spoon the fragility of order, the thin membrane between real and illusory was exposed with a single twist from front to back, back to front, the world would be long and upside down in the hollow of the spoon, squat and right-side up in its outer curve. This made his budding muscles tighten, an exhilaration to come over him that was unlike any other.

He liked to watch dust motes dance in a ray of sunlight. He was moved most deeply by the canal that ran behind the tavern, the constant movement of light on the water seemed to glide along its surface like glowing embers. He felt bliss when watching raindrops engorged with sunlight slide down a window. The curved recurrence of light caught in the hollow of the spoon, between the speckles of rust, thrummed in Manfred's ear like a perfect C note on a violin, entered his narrowed pupils as music illuminated. To Manfred his spoon was an altar of God.

He liked to spin round and round, face towards the sky, eyes squinting at the sun so each beam became snagged on his lashes like bars of gold that seemed to stretch on for ever. But this was always quickly interrupted by his mother. This was second in exhilaration: the frenzied commotion of light and his own perceived manipulation of it. He could just as easily squint into a candle flame until his cheeks stung, enthralled by how its movement stretched into a flickering road. This too his mother interrupted.

Manfred could understand people better than his mother knew but not in any way someone who wasn't Manfred could recognize. He heard the voices of others, though he seemed not to, but for him their voices were muffled, like sounds under water. For him the voices of others were less important than his obsessions with the orders of colour and blissful enormity of light. It could be said he preferred them above all else and, if actions speak louder than words, then, yes, Manfred loved his arrangements more than he loved his mother. Just as Wilhelm loved wine more than his wife and sons, more than himself. Though be reminded that the heart is hidden in one's chest and the declaration of love is not produced by ripping out one's heart to show one's beloved, but by a complex system of speech and action where one must complement the other.

So there were no discernable signs Manfred loved his mother, this was true. However, it was just as true to say there were no discernable signs to say he didn't love her either.

The same could be said about his father and brother. He noticed none of their faults: that his father drank too much wine, that his brother Konrad was nowhere near as beautiful as he was. He did see the way the deep furrows round his father's eyes crinkled when he smiled like miniature, crimson fans, and that in the two pockmarks left over on Konrad's face from illness, one under his left eye and the other, smaller one, in the middle of his left cheek, both pooled with light when they were outside into sparkling dimples, shallow golden ponds.

For Manfred it was when others sang that he best felt a sense of language, when words rose from their muffled depths and their sound and shape gained buoyancy. When sung, words took on a colour. Each note was surrounded by a corona of light that appeared like flower petals, and in the middle, the stamens were the lyrics, so that together it was much the same as what tumbling gerberas would look like.

Colour and light he understood and so, therefore, as long as words were carried on the tide of song he could retain them perfectly and in order. He could recite words as easily as if they were there before him. He saw them like a fan made of the finest peacock feathers and he could readily conjure their linearity, their sequence. It made sense – the order of words, their importance – verbal codes for light and colour he could translate. Each lyric conjured images of dawn or dusk, or the lush green of a rolling pasture after a morning rain, the frenetic rush of the river with its meshwork of luminous butterflies gliding on its surface would rise up before him, a lucid dreamlike landscape. The vibrations in his throat as harmonic words tumbled there, their own gleeful entities that would soon glide and shimmer their way out, dart across the air as disembodied but orderly creatures, was an astonishing sight only Manfred could witness.

Lastly, it should be pointed out, that if you were to think Manfred must have suffered from that childish fear of the dark, you are mistaken, for dark was just the enhancer of light and not an opposing force. Instead, darkness descended like a watery substance that slowly congealed round lightness and colour, like a protective shell, so each could, in Manfred's mind, rest.

They were harmonious, light and dark, not polarities to be utilized as symbols for the battle between good and evil, the faithful and faithless. He lived in a world where such schisms did not take place, where each detail blended into the next, where a gradient of colour and light existed in agreement, each enhancing the other's shade as its brightness bled out and went dim. Nothing clashed, but was symbiotic.

If God is in the details, then Manfred saw God everywhere.

# CHAPTER 8

Elsie stood with her two daughters just inside the tavern door with an offering of warm bread and a satchel of crab apples sticking out of a bucket. Her little one, close to Manfred's age, awkwardly held her infant sister. All their faces were damp from the drizzle that had begun to fall.

'I brought you some bread and apples.'

'Thank you.' It seemed an ominous gesture, a hint of what would come – subsisting on charity. Or could it be a boastful gesture? Elsie's husband was a roofer after all.

'Wretched weather, just wretched. God willing it will clear soon.'

'Have you heard anything yet about the vineyards?' Anna asked this compulsively, she knew Elsie would have heard nothing.

Elsie crossed herself. 'I've heard nothing on the vineyards. But I spoke to Frau Menz, she was out with her husband, boarding a window that had been broken in the storm. Frau Menz said when the hail stopped, she and her mother-in-law went out to collect a hailstone, to see its size. She said she had never seen one of such enormity, it was three times as large as an acorn.' Elsie, likely realizing this was not very consoling, went on, 'But the window was broken by that big tree in front. She told her husband to prune it; he must be sorry for not listening now. So it wasn't the hail that broke it, but the wind.' Elsie said this last part as a sort of retraction to the severity of the hail. She was the sort of woman who spoke first, thought later, but was always sensitive to those about her, even if it was in retrospect.

Anna noticed another bucket and realized, though hail had fallen and their tavern could be in ruins in just a matter of weeks, Elsie wanted to use the tavern water pump. For a moment Anna felt used.

Having a private water pump, was one of the perks of being a tavern-keeper's wife. Having access to water without having to walk to a public pump or to the river where one would have to deal with beggars and crude peasants made Anna rather popular with the other wives living near the tavern.

They would come and ask her if they could fill a bucket or two, to save them the walk. If Anna felt someone was taking advantage of her generosity, she would turn them away. If she suspected that they looked at her oddly, or at Manfred oddly, she turned them away. There were other reasons as well. If a certain wife disliked someone Anna liked, or the other way round, she would turn them away. She took full advantage of her position as keeper of the water pump, and had good excuses as to why the pump was not working and the wife's bucket would have to go unfilled.

It brought out a pettiness in her. She did not realize this in herself at the time, but it was hers to defend and open up to those she preferred; she was empress of the water pump.

The water pump was, of course, mostly a ruse, a way for wives to befriend the tavern-keeper's wife, for what better way was there to find out how much their husbands drank and gambled and what he may have said about his wife? They brought Anna small offerings in exchange, some soup or half a loaf of bread, chicken giblets, or something from their small gardens.

For a moment Anna considered turning Elsie down, just to punish her for her bad timing, but she was one of Anna's closest friends, and the offering of bread and crab apples in exchange for the pump no longer seemed ominous but their common exchange. Out of relief Anna turned round and led Elsie into the kitchen towards the back door, their conversation continued about the treacherous weather. Just as they were about to step outside

Konrad appeared. His curly brown hair was flattened against his forehead.

'You go on, Elsie,' she said, and kept Konrad behind in the kitchen.

Her heart beat faster and pleas to God ran through her mind that the vineyards should be inexplicably unscathed, that God had no interest in testing her just now.

'Inflation is predicted,' Konrad said, with feigned breathlessness as if he had run straight there and back.

'Who did you talk to?'

'A carter.'

'Well, what else did he say? Did he say which vineyards were wrecked? Or how damaged? Did he say how much the price of wine is to go up? What else did he say?'

'Nothing, just that inflation was predicted.'

She let out a frustrated sigh. 'You didn't ask anything else?'

'Why didn't you go then?' He breathed in and waited for her response.

Anna grabbed his arm. 'That's some tongue.' She was angry, but even to herself, her voice sounded insincere and helpless. He was beyond her command.

Manfred suddenly hurried into the kitchen, the turnip flower still in his hand. He went right past Anna and Konrad and out the kitchen door with such determination as if he too were required to deliver some very important news.

Anna let go of Konrad's arm. 'I suppose a carter wouldn't know much yet either.'

He let out a snigger she knew was directed at Manfred and at her failure to discipline him.

Anna swung round towards the open door, looked first at the water pump to see if Elsie was trying to talk to Manfred, then past the pump to the small canal behind the tavern where he sometimes went and where Elsie would see him, but he was not there either. The canal had risen considerably since yesterday, but before this anxiety could take shape, she noticed Manfred crouching down to the right of the door. He seemed content and more importantly, occupied, so Anna let him stay there. She stepped out onto the path of trampled grass that led to the pump. All the grass was flattened, slicked to one side. A sparse rain cooled Anna's cheeks.

Elsie was waiting for her beside the pump, not wanting to fill her bucket until Anna was there, not out of politeness, but to draw out their visit.

'If it had not been so windy last night, I would think it was Juditha who tipped over the rain barrel.'

Elsie would always begin this way, making some statement about Juditha that invited Anna to enquire further. For a moment Anna considered asking whether her husband was still suffering from headaches, just to deflect yet another conversation about Juditha, Elsie's stepdaughter and her preferred subject of discussion, not out of love, however, but because of the suffering she claimed Juditha made her endure.

'Where is Juditha?'

'She was dawdling back there with her bucket. I asked her twice to hurry on, but she walked even slower out of spite. I can't grab her by the arm and drag her, can I? Not when I have a babe in my arms and another at my legs. My own children! I have my own to mind,' she said again, though with more emotion, as if by saying so again and again, that Juditha was not hers that she was indeed only her stepmother, Juditha would somehow become untethered from her husband and float away.

Elsie then relayed Juditha's antics around the household, her uselessness, her fumbling, making things worse for Elsie, sabotaging her all along the way to get out of having to do more. When her husband (he was not ever referred to as Juditha's father) arrived home, Juditha acted so eager to please and help him. Elsie felt Juditha was jealous of her presence and resentful of her husband's other children, though her own mother had been dead since she was seven or eight. It was as if she were taking out some kind of vengeance on Elsie for trying to take her place. Since Elsie had birthed her last baby she had become increasingly focused on Juditha's seeming disregard for her and her own.

In the past Anna would have offered the reaction Elsie wanted – shock and sympathy – but now, since the trouble

86

with Manfred had begun, Juditha's antics seemed just that, infuriating, but at least she was of sound mind and body. She would marry in a few years and be out of Elsie's way for good. Elsie's complaints about Juditha were tedious and perhaps ungrateful considering what God had blessed her with. Anna thought how their friendship had waned in the last two years. In fact, though she still enjoyed being gateway to the water pump, and all the attention that got her, it was no longer the pleasure it once was, for she had to worry constantly that Manfred would come out and do something irregular. It had become a cause of stress to have her neighbours show up at any time and have to scramble to put Manfred away.

Even now, Anna looked at how Elsie's child was able to hold the bucket steady in front of the pump as Elsie began to work the lever and draw the water up. When Anna was near Elsie's little girl, she could see how much was wrong with Manfred. He could not do that, though he was a year older. He would have let the bucket fall to the side and stared into the rush of water, maybe become gleeful at the spill.

Juditha finally emerged from round the corner of the stable, giving a little false run towards the pump, as if hurrying. Her arms and legs went out a little too wildly under her skirt and at her side. The braid in her hair had come loose and fragments of straw were lodged in its slackening folds. But then she slowed, it was more a solitary skip. Anna would always be struck at how childish Juditha was for thirteen, how she clung to girlhood when most girls her age were eager for womanhood.

Elsie began a barrage of chastisements, occasionally looking at Anna as if to say, 'See what I must deal with'. She grabbed the bucket from Juditha's hand making her stumble, and then handed it back to her and pushed her towards the pump.

Once they had left Anna went and picked Manfred up. He was still holding his turnip flower. Some rocks and twigs, carefully placed in separate columns, were before him. He made a fuss, his limbs just beginning their panicky flail whenever he was disrupted from his collections, so she put him down again; she just couldn't be bothered today. Hail had fallen.

She went to the stables and milked the cow. Milk worked better fresh to bleach blood out from the sheets on which the weaver's son had slept.

# CHAPTER 9

Time passed like an animal stalking its prey – slowly. Anna went on with her tasks, cutting vegetables for a stew, smaller than usual as she was sure there'd be less patrons willing to pay for a meal at the tavern, given the circumstance. She held back on the meat as well, using just a single stewing bone for the broth. She took the bloodied sheets off the bed and had Margarethe boil some water, though she preferred to scrub at the stains herself. It was a talent of hers, to remove the worst of all stains, but that was not her only aim; she wanted to be away from the drinking room. She wanted Margarethe to do most of the serving.

Many customers dropped into the tavern throughout the day to share or receive information on the state of the vineyards and other crops. The vineyards were damaged was the general consensus, but how damaged no one could say for sure, not yet. Some people claimed there was talk that the vineyards on the southern slope of the valley had been totally lost, while the northern vineyards were nearly unscathed; some claimed the opposite. There was an over-all sense of hearsay and conjecture. Each had their favoured source, and arguments were quick to arise.

Anna could hear that Wilhelm's two closest friends had arrived: a day labourer who worked odd jobs and had a lazy eye, which drooped all the more wildly after too much wine; and a journeyman gunsmith, whose long coarse beard gave off the stench of sulphur. He was frequently at odds with other journeymen gunsmiths. That was what brought him to Wilhelm's tavern, along with the cheap wine. It was far earlier than their usual time and this dis-mayed Anna because Wilhelm would sit with them and they would spend the rest of the day together in conver-sation, eagerly listening to one another complain, idly discussing all the incoming news. When Wilhelm put forth his best argument, his friends would take a moment to con-sider the validity of his claims and earnestly agree. They always did, and Wilhelm would charge them a lower price for their pitchers of wine. Not that he could do much else that particular day other than sit and talk. He couldn't travel up to the vineyards himself, as it was said that the roads were too muddy to be navigable.

Wilhelm sat with them at the table, and Anna said to Margarethe that she would take out their pitcher. She wanted to hear if they had shown up early because they had some reliable news.

'The hail went right through it, and it sank. The merchant had just filled the whole barge with his order of wine and was docked overnight. He'd left his servants aboard to keep watch.' The gunsmith was speaking very loudly, this dreadful information was his find and he wanted to make his claim on it before it lost its currency.

'It's not true.' The day labourer waved him away.

Anna looked at Wilhelm as she set out their cups. His face was sombre and his shoulders drooped with defeat, but a flush of pink was gaining space on his ashen cheeks as his internal stores of wine became replenished. He could think now, fully grasp that misery loomed near.

'Herr Amman just told me himself. I saw him on the way here. I was sure you would have heard it too by now.' The gunsmith was trying to verify his news but it sounded too desperate.

'And it sunk? All of it?' the day labourer asked. Anna slowly poured wine into each of their cups.

'There's no sign of it, but if you drink from the river today you'll get yourself right drunk!'

'No.' The day labourer again refused to believe it. Others around them were listening and some were refuting the possibility of hail sinking a barge.

'I wager if we were to go down there now, we'd see half the city with their heads in the water. These hailstones were the size of my fist.' The gunsmith held his large fist up to demonstrate, then dropped it on the table for emphasis.

'Then what are you doing here?' Wilhelm asked, and nervous laughter broke out. He was pleased by this.

A short discussion on river barges ensued and Anna retreated into the kitchen.

She was irritated at the gunsmith. She didn't believe a word of it or that he had even heard there was a sunken barge. He was only trying to get some laughs. She thought it a premature pluck at making light of tragedy, considering nothing was known for certain and such jests would only tempt fate. Further she couldn't help but suspect he was also trying to lighten Wilhelm's mood in order to encourage his usual generosity with his wine.

Anna reimmersed herself in the task of ridding the blood from the sheets. It was too difficult to feel reassured one moment by good reports on the vineyards, only to feel shattered an instant later, again and again, yet she couldn't completely shut herself off from it and patiently wait for a stable assessment. So she listened, going to the kitchen door, then returning to the sheets and scrubbing, back to the door, back to the sheets – an uncontrollable pacing. As she predicted, the sunken barge full of wine turned out not to be true, but those who claimed to have gone out and collected a hailstone during the night were all in agreement that they had been the size of a man's fist.

'It all depends on how much longer it rains too,' was a tentative statement which gained clucks of agreement and then further confirmations that it was indeed still raining. Anna listened to the rain patter against the windows, relentlessly steady.

Manfred sat idly on the floor beside the large basin she washed the sheets in, entertained still by the turnip flower though it was now accompanied by some leaves he had picked up, one with a ladybug clinging to it. Manfred flipped the leaf with the ladybug back and forth, bringing it dangerously close to his squinting eye, then put it down on the floor, placing his spoon vertically aligned with the ladybug. He would mother it to death, Anna thought. He did this with insects, but the death was always accidental. She would prefer if he just pinched them like normal boys, stamped on them, severed them in two to see if one half would keep moving. She felt repulsed momentarily, by his gentleness, by his constant state of reverie. Wake up, she wanted to scream at him, just wake up.

As the afternoon went on, the regular patrons stopped coming in and out with as much frequency and stayed to nurse a small measure of wine. None of them had meant to stay so long, as they had lots to do at home; take stock, anticipate, plan a strategy, if indeed a food crisis was imminent. Some left but many stayed longer. There was a kind of collective paralysis. It seemed that to leave the tavern would mean having to face the claims that the hail damage was no longer hearsay and they would bear the full weight of their individual burdens. The rain became an excuse to stay.

The chandeliers had yet to be lowered and lit, so the tavern was suffused in the gloomy daylight entering the windows, with a scattering of candles giving a little more light. This was why Anna barely noticed that the city bailiffs had come in.

The sheets were still soaking, the stains surprisingly stubborn. She was standing by the kitchen door again. It took a moment after they had come into sight, for Anna to become aware that the bailiffs were there and were motioning to Wilhelm.

Her first thought was, how annoying that they had showed up so early. They did not usually come until later and she didn't know yet who was staying that night. She thought the bookseller was staying again, but had not yet seen him that day. The weaver and his son were gone, that she was sure of. What about the peasants? They said they would be returning to the countryside, but the weather may have prevented them. Should she say the peasants were staying another night?

The bailiffs led Wilhelm towards the smaller vacant room once meant to be used for guild meetings. How baffling, Anna thought, that they would go in there. It took but a moment or two to relay the guest information and the bailiffs always made a point of having their presence felt by the patrons. She went towards them. As she approached, she decided only to report the bookseller as a guest. She would send Konrad out later to wherever the bailiffs thought they would be in a couple of hours if the peasants were to return for another night.

Wilhelm's head was lowered, a mannerism of his when he was still sober and aware of how much his breath smelled of wine, and his inability to maintain eye contact for long. Wilhelm and the bailiffs glanced up at Anna as she approached, and fell momentarily silent. A panic swept over her; they knew. They knew about Manfred and were telling Wilhelm. This was not a conscious thought, but it was the source of nearly all Anna's momentary fits of panic. Though maybe on this day it was the fear that the bailiffs had, for some reason, special knowledge about the obliterated vineyards and had come personally to deliver sentence on their tavern that caused her face to pale as it always did whenever confronted with situations where she could not immediately predict their context. Not that it made any sense that the bailiffs would deliver such news.

'Frau Wirth.' The bailiffs moved apart from one another to include her in their small circle.

Wilhelm was squinting, his eyes red; he looked up at her. 'We had a weaver, a Herr Elsasser, stay here last night? Or no?' The odd addition of the negative at the end of his question sounded hopeful, as if Wilhelm could cue Anna into the wanted outcome – that, no, father and son had not stayed at his tavern. 'I should go and get the guest list,' Wilhelm said, though he made no move towards the kitchen where it was kept.

The bailiff had cut him off.

'Our records indicate that one Herr Elsasser and his son, Hans, stayed here last night, do you confirm this?' the taller bailiff asked Anna, in a way that was dismissive of Wilhelm, whose bungling was off-putting.

'Yes.' Anna felt herself relax. This happens, she thought, the weaver was in debt and the bailiffs were here looking for them.

'As I just said to your husband,' Wilhelm was slumped against the wall, looking down at his shoes, 'Hans Elsasser has been arrested for acts of witchcraft, and a warrant for arrest has been issued for Herr Elsasser's apprentice, Georg Scheffel. The charges include acts against nature: sodomy, bestiality, consorting with the devil, acting as the devil's evil doer, and heresy.'

'The apprentice wasn't with them.' She said that defensively, desperately, as if somehow the absence of the apprentice would somehow distance the tavern from this scandal.

'Yes, our records show that. You will both be required to provide a statement in court regarding the actions of Hans Elsasser and to relate any suspicious behaviour that might aide in his prosecution.' A look of excitement spread across his face. Both bailiffs were enlivened by this interruption from their usual tedious task of taking down names of guests and issuing fines. When they returned two hours later to obtain guests' names, they still appeared this way.

# CHAPTER 10

When the bailiffs left the second time, and the bookseller and two peasant guests (who did indeed stay another night) were settled in their rooms, Anna and Wilhelm went to their own room. They walked slowly side by side with a defeated gait. A bouquet of misfortune had been placed in their unwilling hands.

Sleep would not come for hours.

Anna lit more candles than she normally would, until the room seemed ablaze in its ordinariness. They sat upon their unmade bed where Wilhelm had lingered so long that morning that Anna had failed to remember to make it. Now the tussled blankets seemed a comfort. They had woken there and survived the day and could now, successfully, return to it and be ferried off to tomorrow.

Wilhelm was uncharacteristically sober for the late hour, and at first, there was a great enthusiasm between him and

Anna to discuss who they had unknowingly housed in their inn. They were too restless to lie down. 'A witch here? At our tavern!' Wilhelm turned towards her, and then it began, the long discussion of each detail of Hans.

Anna went over what she had heard when she paused in front of Hans' room: the scuffle, how Hans had looked when she set the bowl of oats in front of him, how he and his father had interacted in such a strange way. Everything was a clue now to Hans' true identity. There was a kind of horror-filled giddiness between them. They both felt clever in their careful dissection of their guest, his gestures and expressions, all now appearing very sinister. Wilhelm even said he recalled thinking the night before in the tavern that Hans walked a little stiffly, and this seemed to him a sure sign of sodomy.

She told him about the loud clang of the kicked chamber pot, the slam against the closed door. Wilhelm listened carefully to everything she said, and then asked her to go over some detail again. 'What was his skin like, pale? Witches are said to be pale.'

'Yes, the young man was rather pale.' Hans' face blanched in Anna's memory.

'A witch, here in our very tavern,' Wilhelm, still incredulous, said again.

They both knew it would be just a matter of time before the news spread that a witch had slept, eaten and drank at the Myrrh Tree tavern. Then the tavern would become a place to avoid, furthering the threat of economic despair. He stood and poured himself a cup of wine from the pitcher on the table. She watched and knew he was aware of her watching him, and so he poured but half a cup.

Anna's opinion on witches, up until that night, had been that it was an accepted fact there existed those who were not steadfast in their faith, and were easily swayed by the devil's offerings of easy money or false love, but she had never before directly had an encounter with a suspected witch. There were those rumoured to be witches of course, but still Anna had only seen them from afar and had had no personal dealings with them: the dyer's daughter with her tarry black hair and cleft lip, who supposedly once caused a horse to stop eating and drinking; the once successful seamstress who turned arthritic and had to beg. It was her quick fall into poverty that made her suspicious, for all knew this incited resentment and jealousy and jealousy is the exposed jugular that invites the devil. There was also the very elderly midwife, who was known to undress in front of a window, letting any passer-by have full view of her sagging breasts that hung like narrow, emptied purses so low that her nipples were nearly perfectly aligned with her naval, supposedly in an attempt to render impotency in anyone who caught a glimpse of her.

But mostly witches were a problem of the villages, and

only came to Flusstal to be tried on statements by other villagers and usually executed. In fact Flusstal had never suffered from an infestation of witches like the rest of the Holy Roman Empire. It seemed it was one of the fortunate small pockets of the empire that held firm enough in its faith so the devil never lingered long. The uncovering of large sects of witches always happened elsewhere, and even just the few discovered close to the city were from the villages.

It was something most people in Flusstal felt almost smug about whenever the topic of witches arose in the tavern instigated by a traveller from afar, that in the last hundred years or more there had just been the occasional burning of a witch; five years could pass without any such incident at all.

Instead of sitting next to Anna, Wilhelm pulled the chair up to the end of the bed, resting one leg on it's edge, though this didn't break the intimacy of their conversation.

Anna told him about the streaks of blood on the sheets, and the way the stains seemed to persist no matter how hard she scrubbed, how they seemed to shift in shape like rolling ink.

'I can't think what would make a young man turn that way,' Wilhelm said again. 'And the father, what did he seem like?' and once more they were back at the beginning. In truth this was what they were both most uncomfortable about, that Hans was too much like the ideal young male citizen who toiled under his father's supervision, who was just as likely as any other to marry and produce children and whose children would in turn do the same and populate the empire with other ideal citizens. It was so deeply unsettling to consider that the devil had caught such a productive and future reproductive soul.

They had not talked so much in so long, there was almost a kind of pleasure in it. Anna had stretched her legs out next to Wilhelm's, and almost like children, they went incredulously over this guest with a faulty soul. Both of them seemed desperate not to stop talking, and mocked the superstitions of the villages as if it somehow trivialized Hans' suspected crimes. Of course he would be from the village, of course he would fall into the devil's snares. They guessed at what the devil had offered him. Wilhelm thought it was money, it was always money. Then he said maybe the devil came in the form of a woman, an incubus.

'Could you imagine the very moment when he realized it?'

Not that Wilhelm said this out of sympathy, although by then they could allow themselves to marvel that the witch was so unlike the devil's usual fodder of old women.

'But a sodomite,' Anna said and they both found reassurance in this, that regardless of what the devil offered, Hans had not remained steadfast, but had lost himself in lust. Regardless that Hans was not some forgotten old woman from the margins of the busy, productive world, he was still unlike both Wilhelm and Anna.

They carried on talking for another couple of hours, until Wilhelm could no longer be bothered to pretend to half fill his cup. Anna suddenly realized it was brandy in his pitcher, not wine. She retreated a little more from the conversation each time he sipped from his cup, as if sipping made up for the frequency he brought the cup to his lips. When his speech took on the cyclical quality of drunks, and what was once careful and reciprocated was now a rant, Anna went to bed and pulled the covers over her head. With each drink he took she felt more enfeebled, gone was the feeling of safety they had built up.

She held her rosary. The thinned parts of the blanket let in the lamp's light and made her hands appear pinkish, soft, young.

Anna used to upset Wilhelm in their early years of marriage, when he became fraught with the morning illness wine and brandy brought on, by saying the rosary at the end of the bed, in the very chair he now sat upon. He would tell her to go away, do her praying elsewhere, in church, he said, keep it in the church. But Anna would go on, saying it was him she was praying for and she would watch as the guilt settled over his face and just to get away from her, he would get up. Its effectiveness did not last long, and Wilhelm soon managed to sleep through her prayers, sometimes telling her he actually found it soothing. She knew he was lying, but still he won, and she gave it up.

This time when she began to pray it was to shut out Wilhelm's tedious voice.

'Are you listening?' he periodically called out to her. She answered 'Yes' each time, in the most noncommittal way so as to encourage him into silence and sleep.

Wilhelm however was becoming increasingly more agitated. The more his body slackened under the influence of drink, the more his mind raged against this physical passivity through a confusing diatribe that briefly revitalized him.

'How dare he come to my tavern . . . What will we do, Anna? When none come here because some witch? A *witch*? Took a drink here, a meal here?'

This was another of Wilhelm's drunken traits, to put forward every sentence, even words, with a questioning inflection at the end in an attempt to cover his slurring.

Anna was nearing sleep when finally, in a burst of aggression, Wilhelm leapt from the chair and went angrily down the hall to the room where Hans and his father had stayed. He swung open the door, and stood, teetering at the threshold, then, finally, flung himself forwards. Anna went after him and watched helplessly as he tore back the linens from the bed, kicked through the ash in the hearth, knocked over the flea traps, dragged down the table, spilling the untouched bowl of wine.

He dropped to the floor, looked under the bed and went

perfectly still. He seemed so strangely enormous on the ground, his hands tucked under his chest. For a moment Anna thought he was in pain, that perhaps he was clutching at his chest.

'Anna come.'

He reached out for her hand without looking up. She hesitated, she didn't want to encourage this outburst, and yet she didn't want him waking the guests. She felt a girlish fear bubble up inside her at the thought of looking under the bed, especially one a witch had slept in.

Wilhelm wagged his open hand, 'Come.'

Finally she took it and he pulled her towards the floor.

He was holding the candle dangerously close to the bed so as she knelt she said, 'Careful of the candle, it's too—'

Then she saw what it was he was looking at and slid down beside him.

It was one of Manfred's collections; she could see that by how carefully it was arranged. This was what Manfred did, this is what he saw as he lay next to his lines of leaves or stones. Is this all he sees?

'It is some kind of hex? Some attempt at a pentagram?' Wilhelm slid back, curled up awkwardly into himself.

Anna nearly laughed out loud, she was just about to say it was only one of Manfred's creations, one of his lines. Maybe Wilhelm would also laugh, but that mood was long gone. She couldn't tell him. She couldn't explain why Manfred would arrange leaves in this way under any bed. She lay there a moment, the pressure of the floor against her stomach felt odd and reminded her of being with child.

'I don't know what this is.' As she said it, she quickly grabbed the leaves, much more quickly than Wilhelm's reflex to stop her, got up and ran out of the room and down the stairs. Wilhelm called after her, but it was too late. Anna tossed the leaves in the dwindling fire still burning in the drink room. She had never before feared that Wilhelm would strike her, but when he reached her and grabbed one of her wrists she braced herself for it.

'I will not let any witch's curse put us in jeopardy. I risked myself to be rid of it so I will be the one tainted, not you, if it had any potency. Don't you see? It had to be done and I wished not for you to be exposed.' Anna fell to her knees, leaning her head against his thigh. Never had such melodrama passed between them, never had their emotions run so wildly in one night. Never had they witnessed such combativeness in one another and, when their eyes met, they both felt the possibility that perhaps this was Satan's doing causing such upheaval between them.

Or at least that was what Anna willed her husband to think.

Margarethe stuck her nose out of the kitchen door where her sleeping quarters were, and asked if everything was all right, and so interrupted their dispute.

Wilhelm released Anna, and said only that it was evidence. He stayed by the fire for most of the night, as if to keep an eye on the burning leaves, as if they could scurry back out like lighted hands or skull lanterns.

Four days later when he stood in front of the chief justice to give his statement, he would spare no detail of this leafy pentagram and everyone in the crowded Council House would listen with bated breath. Hans would by then be responsible for a cow that had dried up, the miscarriage of an ironsmith's wife and, of course, the hail and the unrelenting rain (which justified the unusual rapidity with which Hans was tried). Wilhelm would also go on to say that attendance at his tavern had dropped significantly since word had spread that a witch had resided there for a night, and eaten and drunk at his benches.

But it was the pentagram that would seal Hans' fate, for there was nothing more tangible than such a statement from the tavern-keeper, considered the most impartial of witnesses.

'I would have brought along the leaves themselves, if my wife hadn't burned them up in the fire.'

'Your wife is brave,' one magistrate would conclude.

And when Anna and Wilhelm finally left together, Wilhelm would walk ahead of her as he did on the way there, but less eagerly and would eventually slow so that by the time they reached the tavern she was but an arm's length away, and Anna would know she was finally forgiven and that they would no longer have to mill about not talking to one another in their near empty tavern.

Anna climbed the stairs slowly in case Wilhelm called her back, dragging her fingers very lightly against the cool exposed brick as she went up. She felt heavy, reluctant, and paused for a few moments, standing still on the steps, listening to Wilhelm clear his throat, to the scrape of the bench as he pulled it out. In the years to come, Anna would think of this night as another missed opportunity to tell Wilhelm about his son, how easily she could have turned round and sat next to him and said, 'That was our son's leaves, he likes to make designs with leaves and various other items.' She might have even gone so far as to say, 'Much like an artist's palette.' But she let the moment pass, a moment that could have prevented the whole disaster that would follow. For the time being, she consoled herself that Wilhelm was so drunk, he wouldn't remember this tomorrow; he wouldn't remember.

As sleep hovered, making its slow descent upon her exhausted body, Anna was suddenly very certain that Manfred had not been in the room where Hans stayed. No, he had never been there. Anna was suddenly so sure of it. She had been with him nearly the whole day and she could distinctly recall shutting the door to the room after cleaning it. Yes, she could feel the latch in her hand, hear the heavy drag of the door, the imperceptible click as the door met its frame. So when it was her turn to give her statement after Wilhelm, she could be most succinct in its delivery: the noises she heard, the bruises on Hans' face, and the curious nature of the stained sheet. When asked about the leaves she needed only to say that there were leaves, but that because her reaction to them was so quick, she could say nothing more but that she felt it was very important to burn them.

# CHAPTER 11

In total there were six churches in Flusstal, but the Holy Cross was the largest in size and congregation. It was high up the hill, and so its spires could be seen from nearly anywhere in the city. It was built in the late fourteenth century and had been crowned with two openwork spires that appeared to sway against the sky, especially on a windy day when the clouds moved at a perceptible speed. If one were to pause a moment and look directly up before entering the church it seemed likely that the spires would tumble down upon one's head. It was an unnerving experience, but one that was strangely compelling for children entering the church with their parents, as if this perceptual swoon of the spire confirmed God's love for them by not falling, while at the same time engendering enough uncertainty to evoke fear and make them thoroughly reticent upon crossing the church threshold. It was a fleeting fear and disappeared as soon as the spires could no longer be viewed. One was left feeling slightly dull in the wake of such anxiety, but there was also the childish disappointment that the spires remained intact, and the curiosity about what would happen if they were to fall was unresolved.

Manfred never fussed in church and for this Anna was grateful. He stayed perfectly still, perfectly fixed upon the myriad of stained-glass windows depicting biblical scenes surrounded with banderols and plant arabesques. Even without the sun, the windows beguiled him. He was entranced each Sunday by Mary at the loom, the epic of Jonah inside the belly of a whale, Eve's seduction or the brilliant scourging of Christ. While the organ was being played and the choir sung hymns, Manfred would keep his eyes on the windows, but the look of concentration on his face intensified and Anna would wish she could hear his thoughts. She never had to worry about him during the service, it was afterwards, when trying to lead him out of church while all the other children tottered eagerly away, that he was errant, squirming out of her reach to stay in the pew close to the windows.

There had been six more days of rain; the skies stayed grey as slate. The clouds hung low and seemed to have congealed into an immovable gristle stuck to the bloated belly of the sky. It was no wonder everyone believed the sky was falling. The rain only took brief pauses, as if preparing behind the clouds for its next performance: a slanted rain, a heavy rain, sparse rain with fat drops, dense rain with fine drops, an undulating mist, rain that fell so swiftly it seemed to bounce off the ground just to go up and fall back down again. There was every kind of rain although it did not hail again, but this was a mercy no one noticed, already too wearied by the onslaught of rain, by the oddness of its patterns, by its punitive quality. In fact it seemed the whole city was trapped in an endless, bluish dusk, a purgatory of sunlessness.

The church smelt of damp bodies and mildewed clothes which the thurible being swung by Father Gottlieb could barely mask as his procession approached the altar. The hem of his alb skimmed the stream of muddy prints that ran down the middle aisle.

Father Gottlieb was young and amiable, especially gifted in his use of story and parable to convey to his congregation the word of God. He prefaced Bible readings with theological questions, then delved into the most ordinary, everyday anecdote – some exchange in the market, even just the purchasing of bread, could lead him to make an observation relevant to Matthew or the Book of Revelation, any reading at all. God seemed all the more accessible this way, all the more omniscient, and this resulted in a congregation all the more secure in their faith.

His antiphon was also quite pleasant to listen to.

His tenor voice took on an easy conversational style as he

began the homily. Even his narrow shoulders seemed to ease, and his long fingers lay flat and relaxed on the podium.

'In Isaiah, the Lord says, "I will wash you as clean as snow. Although your stains are deep red, you will be as white wool. If you will only obey me, you will eat the good things the land produces. But if you defy me, you are doomed to die. I the Lord, have spoken." What must one relinquish in servitude to God?'

Father Gottlieb looked out towards his congregation, letting so much time pass that one almost felt compelled to answer him.

'A man came to the church the other day and said to me "Father, my son has committed a mortal sin, and I am worried that God has lashed out. I lament that my son's transgression has led God to unleash his anger on all the land. What should I do?"' Father Gottlieb was also adept at changing his voice so that it was easy to distinguish between speakers. He could even produce accents, though on this day he gave the man's voice a bleating pitch.

'I told the man that Job's faith was tested when the devil destroyed his children and his crops. I told him it is the sins of the parents that leave their children open to attack: cursing, coveting, gambling, drunkenness, poor church attendance. These are windows through which the devil enters.

'"But my son is no child," said the man, "and I am more faithful than most men."'

113

'I reminded him that Job's children were not swaddled babies, but grown men when Satan came for them. I asked him what sin his son had committed? At this the man wept, and in a near inaudible croak, he said, "Sodomy."'

'Sodomy.' Father Gottlieb said it again. Gone was the conversational style from a moment before, in its place was a mixture of incredulity and indignation emphasized by his sudden increase in volume. 'Sodomy: a sin most abhorred by God. You must turn your son in, I implored him, let his fate rest in God's hands. It is His will and you will be exonerated. Sodomy, I told him, is the work of the devil, for the devil will always try to rub out what God has made. God created man and woman, they are to become one flesh, to replenish the earth. Satan attacks this, just as he attacks crops. Your son has fallen to Satan's wiles.'

His voice, rising, rising, so that each listener was surging with indignation. Each listener felt carried off in the tide of his voice.

'At this the man cried further. "But I love him."' A whiny sound, so that one could only picture the man to be effeminate as well.

Again, silence. 'Just as God loved his son.' There it was – the unarguable. He had the man there, no rebuttal existed.

'"I will turn him in, Father." The man wept.

'"Where is your son?" I asked him.

'"He is waiting for me outside."'

'"Turn him in and I promise you now, that I will minister to his soul in prison, so that he can atone and save his soul from eternal damnation."'

Gratitude swelled in everyone there. Oh, how he wanted to save the land and vineyards, how he wanted to save us.

'This man's son, this weaver's son, this *witch*,' *witch* was the final crescendo and had its intended impact, with a rush of praises to God unfurling like a heavy fog from the mouths of all there, 'was seduced by the devil and, though we suffer for it, we will drive out the wicked, and God's grace will be returned to us.

'You may have once believed that witches were a village problem, and it is exactly this slackening in vigilance against evil that has brought God's wrath down upon us. The hail, the rain is not just a village problem now, is it? It is here because God brings sorrow for sins committed.'

He returned now, to the easy speaking style. 'What must be given up? The answer is everything. Just like Job, all that we hold precious, all that we love can be taken, but still we must believe in the path God sets for us, and in this we will prosper, here or in the heavenly kingdom above. In the name of the Son, the Father and the Holy Spirit, amen.'

Anna remained kneeling after Mass, letting the crowd inside the church thin out before attempting to rouse Manfred. She let Konrad and Caspar go out before her then took Manfred to the statue of Mary and lit a candle. She found the subtlety of candlelight allowed Manfred an easier adjustment from inside the church to outside, that a gradual departure worked best to prevent any flailing objections he might have and if he were to have an outburst at least the church was near empty. She prayed that the vineyards could be salvaged, that Wilhelm would turn away from wine, that customers would return to the tavern and that Manfred would speak soon. She picked Manfred up, and he flung his head back to gaze up at the vaulted ceiling that still seemed to echo with the organ's music in its stony ribs. She allowed these last glances of his, pausing briefly by the row of the three attached confessional booths. The curtains were pulled back on the two end booths but not the middle which was no longer used since it had been discovered that the thinned rotting wood allowed one confessor to overhear another through the shared walls and confession for some, became a sort of entertainment and source of gossip. This happened in her mother's day when there were two or three priests running this parish, but still the middle booth remained closed, it was said, as a reminder of the detriments of gossip.

Finally as they approached the doors, Anna put Manfred down and walked with her hands on his shoulders, her own legs propelling him forwards.

Father Gottlieb stood outside by the doors, giving the feel of a hospitable host seeing off his guests and perhaps trying to overhear the impression they were leaving with.

As Anna stepped from the church she was dismayed that of all the moments for the rain to take one of its brief breaks, it had to be then, when the women lingered near the doors, as always, and let their children run off to be occupied with one another, while they shared news of sisters and aunts, new babies, baptisms and marriage unions.

She led Manfred partway down the steps and left him to sit there, where he was hidden to some extent by everyone's lingering legs. It was only ever for a few minutes because as the tavern-keeper's wife, she always had ample excuse to go off sooner than the others; Sunday was the busiest day at the tavern.

Today, though, no one paid Manfred any attention, nor did Anna have to get back so quickly owing to their lack of customers. Only the gunsmith came regularly, and this was bad, for then Wilhelm and he would spend the evening trying to drink a barrel empty, with the gunsmith encouraging Wilhelm's self-despair.

Today, the steps were filled with the same nervous incessant chatter that Wilhelm and Anna had experienced a few nights ago. Though she wanted not to be Anna was swept in by the questions from the other women and reiterated her court statement. Of course, she too felt feverish after the sermon, and so perhaps drew out the facts of Hans' stay, embellishing them here and there. She found she couldn't help it.

★

117

Konrad tried to lose Caspar behind the church. Caspar stupidly thought their game on the way to church would continue. They had taken turns discreetly trying to trip one another up behind Konrad's parents' backs. If either his mother or father turned back to look, they had to make up a reason for their stumbling, 'Ah, a big twig' or simply recover from their near fall quickly enough for it not to be noticed.

Konrad didn't want to be seen with the cellar boy on that particular Sunday. He was inconsistent in this; on some days he was quite happy to rollick around with Caspar, losing himself and his embarrassment of being seen with the cellar boy in a game of mercenaries. Today he felt particularly conscious of his attire, and thought it too closely matched Caspar's Sunday clothes in quality. It was a terrifying prospect for him to be mistaken for a servant. He had also become very mindful of how he smelt, or thought he smelt as he'd become so accustomed to the scent of manure. Before church, he would rub a piece of leather against his chest and hair in the hope of masking the odour.

Caspar jumped up behind him, so that his shoulder smacked against Konrad, but rather than stumble dramatically forwards, Konrad elbowed him in his stomach.

'Stop it,' he said, and went off alone in the other direction.

Behind the church, Konrad usually fulfilled his longing to move during the ceremony by running, jumping, wrestling anyone willing. Behind the church was an oasis for the children, an alternative world to the adult one, where they were able to go and exercise their flexible bodies and step into imaginary worlds.

Even though he was one of the oldest boys still romping around here, rather than inspire awe Konrad was often considered an annoyance by many of the children. Though he suspected this was what others thought of him, he could not curb how wound up he became, how roughly he would play and he seemed unable to stop inviting himself into others' games. He would purposely walk in front of someone's rolling hoop after they finally had it spinning with their stick, though he would claim not to have seen it. The moment Konrad felt resented, he often tried to redeem himself, telling the boy he had just released from a headlock that he was stronger than he looked, or that someone's hoop was nicer than any other he'd seen, or generally attempt some funny, contorted stumble to make the other person laugh. This made him just that bit more unlikable, for he wasn't exclusively intimidating which left him open to ridicule when he had turned the other way.

He would try desperately to control himself, but somehow he couldn't. It was as if everything inside that felt so bound up from Monday to Saturday became unfettered in a surge of uncontrollable force that propelled his arms and legs along.

Today he was very mindful of how he carried himself. He

walked slowly with a kind of slouching, warding off his temptation to gallop around.

He was hoping the fact that the witch had stayed at his tavern would win him some acclaim. Konrad contrived a casual walk and brooding disposition. His slow pace was designed to attract questions from others; he wanted to be perfectly accessible at all times. He circled round the small groups who were standing talking about the witch, just like their parents in the front. There weren't any games being played, aside from the very young half fighting over a leather ball.

When no one seemed to notice him, he strolled near Juditha's group of girls.

'Tell us, Konrad, what happened?' She broke away from her group of younger friends. If Konrad hadn't been so desperate to be asked this, he might very well have ignored her as he usually did. Juditha was not the sort of girl one wanted to be known to have affection for, being not very pretty with her long, thin face, and her ill-fitting dress and scraggly braids. She also should no longer be going here to play. Konrad would often reassure himself with this. She only got away with it because her toddling stepsister was there. But she didn't stand at the margins of things as her peers did, quietly watching over her stepsister, ready to prevent any bad falls or break up quarrels between tots, appearing to be above the chaos in the narrow tract of dead grass and cobblestone and her other stepsister, the infant, was never left in her care, freeing her up to do as she wished. For this she was an object of derision from girls her own age and so took refuge in the company of those younger than her. There she could be the leader, but it seemed to stifle her growth both physically and mentally. Often she spoke with the same puerile cadence of her younger friends.

Usually Juditha was engaged in biblical re-enactments. Just last Sunday she was playing Easter. She urged a boy to lie down as if he were dead and then she and three other girls circled round him dropping flowers near him, at which point he was suddenly resurrected and chased them as they screamed gleefully.

The attentions of the girls attracted interest from some of the boys, and soon Konrad held the attention of a large assembly. It quickly went round, for those who didn't know, that the witch had stayed at his father's inn. Konrad revelled in the attention, and felt a flush of gratefulness towards Juditha. He promised himself not to act so irritated by her growing visits to the stable.

'His horse acted funny,' he started, 'bared his teeth and tried not to let him on.'

'Cos he's a bugger!' A boy with blackened gums hooted with laughter.

More laughter ensued from those crowded round. Konrad felt perturbed that the other boy had stolen the climax of his story, which he never meant to be funny but serious and disturbing.

Konrad tried quickly to recover their attention. 'That was after, though. I saw him fly down into the cellar trying to get at my father's wine.' The mention of flight quietened them down. 'It was just me and cellar boy there.' He sought out Caspar, nodding in his direction. Some turned and looked, wanting Caspar to verify this, and for a moment it seemed he wouldn't and Konrad felt sorry he told him off before, but then, finally, Caspar nodded.

'We tried to stay perfectly still so he wouldn't notice us, but I couldn't have him drinking down my father's stock, what with the hail. No, I couldn't let it happen. I picked up a jar, planning to throw it and scare him off, but he heard, and took no time to see us. Though it was pitch black.' Right away Konrad corrected this inconsistency. 'I mean, it went pitch black the moment he saw us, but for one candle. So I threw the jar, which had brandy in it, right in his direction, ran for the candle and threw that. He lit up, and made that screaming, popping sound like a grasshopper does when you throw it into the fire.' Konrad would later congratulate himself for this fine comparison. 'He ran out, screaming, but when I saw him the next day, he hadn't a burn on him.'

A rush of questions ensued, and with each answer Konrad was able to refine his story. He ignored the one boy who asked what he was doing in the cellar in the first place, if they had a cellar boy.

But then suddenly the other children were running away

from him. He stopped speaking and could hear the loud staccato shouting coming from the front of the church.

It seemed at first a gentle wind had come up, a warm wind that gently licked the ears of everyone on the church steps, and of the men on the walkway below. The kind of wind that carries on it the distant sound of chimes, or the slight whistle as it goes over an open empty bottle. A simple trick the wind often likes to play. But it wasn't the wind. It took on a cadence, a soft susurruation that at first seemed an undercurrent of the conversation at large, but then diverged and became separate. Its unusual hushing sound silenced those on the church steps and on the walkway. In the absence of their voices it gained strength, took shape. It was now silent but for the song, people were turning round, looking for its origin.

> *Thou comest in the darksome night*
> *To make us children of the light,*
> *To make us in the realms divine,*
> *Like Thine own angels, round Thee shine.*
> *Hallelujah!*

> *All this for us Thy love hath done;*
> *By this to Thee our love is won;*
> *For this our joyful songs we raise*
> *And shout our thanks in ceaseless praise.*
> *Hallelujah!*

Was it the sun that made Manfred sing? He must have been missing its presence, the commotion of the sun's rays, he must have been tired of the dullness round him, tired of the rain, and when he felt the first inklings of the sun's warmth and light, he broke out into song. He rejoiced. Did he feel the sun before anyone else, did he feel its warmth crawl over his arms, did those pores on his smooth hairless arms pucker up? Did he have an innate instinct of the travels of clouds and sense they were parting above him, that the pirate clouds were finally setting the sun free? Did the sunlight manifest itself before him in another way, so he had a vision of the sun breaking through just seconds before it showed? Or did he bring the sun out? Did he draw it out with his voice, in that moment with the whole parish as witnesses. It seemed possible that he alone spoke to God.

The sun hit the back of Manfred's head, his hair shimmered and took on the white-gold shade it did under direct sunlight. The sun, fully unshackled, burned brightly and tumbled down his cheeks. Tumbled down the cheeks of everyone there. And the way Manfred's hair was brushed against his forehead, his serious look, those pristine blue eyes taking up so much of his face was too much for anyone to resist. A seraph was there before them.

The people stilled, opened up, then converged round the song's origin. Round the seraph with his elbows leaning against the step above the one he was sitting upon, his sunlit face tilted towards the sky. Great affirmation was felt just then of God's plan; this child sang on a Catholic church's steps and not a Protestant church up the river in a Protestant city.

The wind turned warm, and filled with promise of plump juicy grapes.

'*Hallelujah! Hallelujah!*' the people on the church steps sang back.

'*Hallelujah! Hallelujah!*'

Manfred brought up his hand to cover one ear and tilted his head to the left to press his other ear against his shoulder, this was not a gesture of rejection for those singing hallelujah round him, but a show of his single-mindedness.

He simply kept singing to himself.

Someone said there was an angel singing on the front steps. All the children ran to the front of the church. An angel. Along the way, this rumour gained speed as they were met with jubilant cries. It was a strange sight to see their parents ensnared in song, in an incantation, as if they could not break from it by their own will. They were a whorl of upturned faces, pressed in together. When some of the children went up the steps to be near their mothers or fathers, they were met with loving embraces.

Konrad felt someone bump into him and he knew it was Juditha taking the opportunity to press gingerly into his back. He could feel her small pointy breasts against him.

He moved forwards away from her. It was fine in the stable, but never out in the open.

All the children from behind the church were now at the front, at the base of the steps. Father Gottlieb had his arms raised to the sky.

Konrad didn't need to see who it was; he knew who was at the centre. He could distinguish his brother's voice from all the others.

It was Manfred.

It was only Manfred.

It was always Manfred.

Anna tried to push through the crowd circling round Manfred, lunge for an arm, even a leg to burrow her son into her skirt, tuck him away. But she could not get through. The enthusiasm of the people overpowered her, made a chain around the child that shut her out. 'Stop it, stop,' she hissed towards Manfred very quietly, not wanting to cause a scene; of course she was not heard. She tried her best to manoeuvre her way towards her son, but she still could not reach him. Oh, how stupid he will look, so oblivious to all the people gathered round him.

In her desperation to reach him, she didn't notice that it seemed as though Manfred was the conductor of the clouds urging them to part further with his song. *'Hallelujah! Hallelujah!'* he sang on, evenly, undisrupted by the frantic chorus round him, *'Hallelujah! Hallelujah!'* Someone's elbow caught Anna's nose, her eyes watered and she staggered slightly back. She noticed Elsie crying, tears of joy streaming down her face. In fact many people were crying, a release of joy and buried sadness came over the whole congregation, even men were wiping their cheeks.

Anna could not say afterwards how it all finally settled, how she was finally able to pick Manfred up. Many people circled round them, touching Manfred's warm back, gliding their hands over his hair. He didn't like to be touched so much and started to writhe in Anna's arms. She held him tightly, to stop his flailing, which caused him to cry. People thought he was tired now, his small body so wrung out from song, and a soothing hush went over the steps.

Wilhelm was finally beside Anna and took Manfred from her and put him up on his shoulders. He did it in pride, but it also, Anna thought, fortunately made Manfred more awkward to reach and so he quieted. A private smile still played over his lips, as if he knew more than those round him, or perhaps he only liked the way the sun wove itself through Wilhelm's wig, the crimson red of it long ago faded came alive again.

'Herr Wirth,' Father Gottlieb, his cheeks pink and lively, his lips twitching with excitement, 'I am going to the prison tomorrow. I think it would benefit the young weaver's soul immensely for your son to accompany me and sing this hymn to the prisoner.'

Wilhelm smiled, very pleased. 'Of course, Father, anything we can do.'

'No,' Anna shouted on reflex. 'No,' she said again, more calmly but the damage was done, everyone was looking at her. She quickly felt herself shrink, turn fluid, her fear of criticism further compounded by the faces looking upon her, waiting for her to provide a reason for this selfishness.

'He has a gift, Frau Wirth, a God-given gift that has presented itself to us today. Would you deny this? He has been called on by God himself. It is clear now, that it was not coincidence that the witch's path crossed with yours. God has called on you as well. Would you deny this?' His voice broke slightly at the end and sounded hurt, personally slighted.

'Of course not, Father, my wife is just acting from a mother's fear that Manfred could be vulnerable to the witch's wickedness.' Wilhelm glanced at Anna as if she were someone he did not really know.

Father Gottlieb went on to assure her that Manfred would have no physical contact with the prisoner and that he would be with him each and every moment. There was nothing she could do, no way to refuse him, not there in front of everyone on the church steps.

Arrangements were made for the priest to collect Manfred from the tavern the next afternoon.

'Bless you and your son.'

★

When Father Gottlieb arrived for Manfred the following afternoon, Anna told him that unlike yesterday on the church steps Manfred usually waited for someone else to start a hymn before joining in, after which point he could sing solo. He didn't know the titles of hymns either, but once the hymn was begun he would recognize it. She went over the hymns he knew best. She also told him that Manfred was not one for severe or sharp noises, so if one of these witches were to make some kind of awful howling, he would very likely cover his ears. Nor did he like to be touched suddenly, his skin was sensitive, best to offer your hand gently, if at all.

Just like that, Anna offered the priest her son.

Just like that, without knowing it, she gave him away.

# CHAPTER 12

Hans would never weave again, at this thought he almost
laughed out loud. His thumbs had been crushed by thumb-
screws, and they were now only flattened stubs, writhing,
beheaded slugs, thin as a page in a book. Georg would
probably never weave again either, for this Hans was sorry.

He couldn't see his hands at all now, there was too
much blood in his eyes and, anyway, his arms had been
pulled up over his head, so that his whole body hung from
them. He was sure his arms were dislodged from his
shoulders and he feared that they had completely broken
away from him, that if he looked up he would see his arms
hanging and he would be on the ground, as he couldn't
feel them anymore. He'd lost consciousness about a half
hour earlier. They had left him alone just before he passed
out. The magistrates. They had left and he was alone. The
only person in the room was the scribe who was there to

take notes of anything Hans said or did. He was waiting for Hans to incite the devil, cry out a lament to his fellow witches to brew him up some concoction and set him free. They left him alone like this for long periods so that there was no distraction from the pain of each broken bone, piece of torn flesh, the sting of the vinegar poured onto his squashed thumbs, or from the short metal rod shoved into his rectum, which they had promised would be replaced with something larger each day until he confessed or until his intestines fell out – whichever came first.

Hans knew it was a forest warden who had seen them. It was the forest warden who told Hans' father what his son and his apprentice were doing together in the woods. This was revealed to him, not by his father, but by the magistrates. At least Hans knew, and now that he did, he wasn't sure why it meant so much to him. It wasn't so much who had found out about him and Georg, but he wanted to know how the forest warden had expressed what he'd seen, what words he had used.

If he had slept with his shirt on at the inn, none of this would have happened. His father might have ignored the forest warden's accusation, dismissed Georg and they would have moved on. He had actually paused and considered keeping his shirt on, because it had been cool in the run-down room. Fine cracks round the window, like varicose veins, had let the air in. In the end, he took off his shirt out of habit; he didn't like to be too warm at night. If he had kept his shirt on, his father never would have seen the bite mark Georg had left in the slope between his neck and shoulder.

It happened when the hail started. They were both woken and Hans had gone to look out of the window. His father had grabbed his hair and flung him into the door. 'I knew it,' he hissed into the back of Hans' head. 'You fucking bugger.' Then, 'My son is a fucking bugger,' as if he were announcing it to some invisible audience, as if he could no longer address Hans directly. Hans was completely astounded, and though his father had called him a bugger, he had no idea why his father was hitting him; he had yet to absorb that he was the bugger in the room. Then he had run his fingers over what he had thought was a bruise and felt the indentations of Georg's straight white teeth.

Where was his father now? At home likely, sitting by the fire. Maybe he had a blanket across his legs. He would still be working on the Hauff order. He probably felt the loss of Georg's workmanship, but not of Hans.

His interrogators had said he committed sodomy with the devil, but it was not Georg who was cast as the devil. The devil was a goat with a long tail, who stood on two legs and Georg and Hans took turns bending over for him. When Hans was insistent that this was not so, they said the devil must have taken the shape of a woman, and Hans and Georg took turns with her, having lost themselves to lust.

132

The latter would be what Hans finally agreed to; it was better than with a goat. When they pressed him to make their narrative his own, stamp it with his own personality, Hans still described Georg: soft dark hair, good teeth, smooth skin.

Hans knew it was a complete fiction. If they had said to him that Georg was the devil in disguise, he would have immediately agreed. He had always thought Georg could be the devil. Why else would he have bent over as he did, let himself be so subdued by him? After all, he found himself completely powerless near Georg.

Finally he was released, and brought back to his cell. The torturer cleaned his wounds, and Hans managed to ask him, 'Why do you do it?'

He meant why had the torturer bothered to clean him, when the next day he would undo his nursing by inflicting more injury. But the torturer didn't answer.

Hans was still floating on the surface of consciousness when the priest appeared in his cell later that morning. The same priest his father had gone to, so he could hear what he wanted to hear – that it was righteous to accuse his own son of witchcraft. He came in with a three-legged stool and a Bible, and sat on the other side of the room. He had good weaving hands, long and spindly. Hans tried his best not to answer any of the priest's questions; but finally he cried out, 'You're wrong, everyone is wrong. I am not a witch.'

The priest answered, 'I only advised your father from the information he gave me.'

Hans took this to mean that the priest was open to his version of events, that he could be swayed to Hans' side.

He was nothing like Hans' frenzied interrogators. The priest was calm and empathetic. He helped establish a routine: Hans' torture and interrogation began each day at dawn, the priest came to see him soon after in his cell before the midday meal was served, then Hans was taken back to be interrogated again and then the priest returned again in the early evening.

He read passages from the Bible, and asked Hans about everyday trivialities. Did he like weaving? What did he like to weave best? From here, Hans revealed his inferiority to Georg, and his overall inadequacy when it came to weaving. The priest said that it was jealousy that gave the devil the best entry to the soul. He asked about Georg. Suddenly Hans could imagine himself with Georg in their despicable act. Hans did not lie about the act that passed between him and Georg. He confessed because he so wanted to pay penance and be forgiven. He was willing to fast, to offer the rest of his life to charity.

The priest pressed him for every minute detail. 'How were you bent? Did your anus tear? Was his member cold or hot? Long or short? Were there any secretions?' Guiding him to questions on the devil, 'Was he tall or short?'

Then he would rephrase everything Hans had said about

Georg. Hans could see how much he'd desired Georg because his father preferred him. He wanted to be Georg because he was so jealous of him.

Then the priest asked about the day his father hired Georg. How close was his father with Georg? Why did it seem his father preferred him over his own son? Was it only coincidence that his father presented his son with a seducer? Could it be that his father was also seduced by Georg?

He brought forth what Hans had suspected all along, ever since his arrest – that it was his father's fault. If he had never taken in Georg, if he could have focused more on bettering Hans' skills, if he had never constantly applauded how great a weaver Georg was, Hans would not be here. His body would not now be torn, his hands would not be mangled. It was his father's fault. If he had never hired Georg none of this would have happened. It was his fault.

Hans must have fallen asleep because when he woke the priest was gone. The light on the ceiling was slanted in a way he knew meant it was afternoon and his torturer had yet to come for him. Hans thought how funny it was that he used the possessive 'his' torturer, as if they were old friends or lovers. He was left in a state of uneasy waiting, each clink, each scuffle made him think that his torturer was coming for him.

The priest returned later in the afternoon, but this time

he didn't come into Hans' cell. This time he had a young boy with him, whom Hans couldn't see, only hear. He sang a hymn for Hans through the door, and Hans knew he would die.

He cried at the sound of this child's ethereal voice, it was as poetic as the sight of a single wispy cloud travelling across a starry night sky. He cried until everything seemed to come loose inside his body – his ribs and spine all fell loose. He cried until his soul expelled what Georg had left inside him. He cried until his soul was recovered and he knew he would confess. He cried until he could cry no more.

Hans could accept it now, he had wronged God and he had to die.

Finally he understood. There were two ways to leave this world: saved or unsaved. Hans would be saved. And, he hoped, so would Georg, so they would be in heaven, together, for eternity.

Before leaving, the priest whispered in the most sympathetic way, 'They will just keep breaking you, my son.' Then he and the child were gone.

When they brought Hans back to the torture chamber, before they could inflict any more pain, he confessed. It took hours. Each time he veered off from an acceptable confession they filled him in, until he arrived at the place they described: the witches sabbat, where a frenetic sexual orgy took place.

'. . . he thrust until something wet and warm poured into me . . . it did not hurt . . . Satan's member was cold as ice . . .' The rain did indeed become wet kisses from others in attendance. '. . . in a writhing orgy like snakes mating in a pit. It happened weekly. They plotted to overturn all that was upright. The devil wore black and drank from a hollowed-out goat's horn. He did not wear shoes.' These were the details they wanted so desperately, these were the details they hoped would make the devil easy to recognize.

'When did Georg first bring you to the devil's sabbat to be initiated by the devil?'

'It wasn't Georg.'

At this he was slapped, his interrogators sighed with frustration, all their progress undone. If he was still protecting the other witch then he had not yet been released by the devil, more torture would be necessary to free him from this wickedness. It could take days, weeks.

'It was my father.'

# CHAPTER 13

Nearly all the residents of Flusstal gathered to watch the burning of Hans, his father and Georg just outside the city's north wall. There was an overall sense of revelling in outrage, a final chance to air their ire, vent their frustration. Shouts filled the air, between which conversations were carried on with the person one was standing next to. Creative insults garnered a bit of nervous laughter, usually to do with sodomizing goats, or men acting as women.

Anna had never been one to attend executions, simply because the tavern filled soon after any such punishment and it would be too troublesome to return in time and have food ready and the wine casks tapped. She had no interest in watching criminals die just for the sake of it, as many did. She went to see Manfred. Father Gottlieb said his singing would help guide the convicted, who had each confessed and expiated their sins, sending them towards salvation.

Not only that, said Father Gottlieb, but for the people, for all those who had suffered because of these witches, it was a time for rejoicing in this victory of good over evil.

It was Wilhelm who agreed and then, later, when Anna pleaded with him not to let Manfred do this performance, he tried to pacify her by saying it would be the last time he'd have to and to think of how the tavern would fill after the witches were dead. 'Everyone's already saying it will be so.'

Anna looked round at all the people there and wondered, How will he do it? How will he sing here in front of all these people? There was too much to distract him, or maybe after he was led out to the platform, he would just keep walking in the other direction, or stumble totally unaware of what he was meant to do. What if he stopped singing suddenly to pick up some spotty insect that just happened to be travelling near his foot? Oh, let this be over, soon. Let it be over. She visualized leaving, she thought only of that moment when she could take Manfred's hand and leave. Let it go smoothly, she pleaded to God.

Konrad felt tremors of self-satisfaction, as if he really had played a role in bringing these witches to justice. This was how he went over in his mind the story he had told behind the church, adding more elaborate details here and there, reworking the logistics of how the witch flew into the cellar. He suspected that others in the elated crowd noticed him and were likely nodding to the person next to them to point him out. He stood a little straighter, and made his stance wider. Maybe he would one day be a city bailiff, rather than a mercenary. This was something to think about.

He and Casper pushed their way to the front.

In full view, in daylight, witches were not much to fear with their skinny bodies; purple and yellow bruises; wounds still seeping, emphasizing the shocking white of their stomachs and upper thighs. The hair on Hans' legs was light, his penis barely poked out from the shroud of much darker hair round it, as if it were the fleshy snub nose of some burrowing animal. The other two men had been shaved, in search of the devil's mark. Hans had been saved this humiliation by Georg's bite mark. It seemed unnecessary to search for further evidence – this had been explained in the onslaught of woodcuts and broadsheets that were posted in the tavern.

At first Konrad studied the witches' faces, looking for a common link, something visibly evident that he himself could look out for and report if necessary, but it was difficult to deduce what their expressions were. As the magistrate read their list of crimes Konrad could not help but be constantly drawn to examining the witches' members. This base curiosity seemed to be something he could not help, and as much as he tried to convince himself that he was not in fact looking there at all, he still found himself comparing the three penises, the slight variations in size and shape; the shaved bodies allowed for greater insight. They should look different somehow after being inside the devil, he thought, they should be emitting steam and appear red hot. Then he started to compare them to his own, to deduce what was to come and how he would develop. He played a little mental game, that he was shopping for one, and had to choose between the three to have one as his own. He chose Georg's because it appeared to him to be the thickest.

'Today, the third of September 1664, Herr Elsasser, his son, Hans, and his apprentice, Georg Scheffel, will die by strangulation, then their bodies will be burnt for their offences against God by signing a pact with the devil, engaging in sodomy with the devil, committing bestiality at the devil's will, for causing harm to the city and people by conjuring a storm through their perverse acts. Herr Elsasser has also been found guilty of inducting his son and his apprentice into the devil's fold, and attending the witches' sabbat where he witnessed two other villagers, Herr Laumayer and Herr Zwenk, who are both already in custody . . .'

The reading of crimes went on, but Hans had stopped listening. His father had taken two more down with them. His father had always disliked those two, both had cheated him on a bill they owed. One was a drunk, the other, Herr Zwenk, a gambler. Hans tried to glance over at his father but gave up the moment the leather straps that tethered his neck and forehead cut into his skin. He didn't really want to see him again and he didn't want to see him tethered to a stake because of his own accusation. Like father, like son, he supposed. It was Georg he twisted his neck for and could partially see. Georg returned his look, and they stayed this way, until he heard the dry gurgling come from Georg's throat, the desperate attempts to gasp for air, until he had to turn away from Georg's buckling knees.

He thought again of how they had wrecked Georg's beautiful body, plundering it with whips and pincers, screws and racks. That was his last cohesive thought. He began a series of frantic prayers that he mumbled as he heard the executioner approach. As the rope tightened round his own neck, held by thick hands in black leather gloves, he heard the boy singing and, as his last breath left him, he felt himself being carried away on this child's voice to a waiting chariot.

As people began to return to their workshops by foot in an excited, jaunty procession, many jokes were passed round, and there was an overall feeling of accomplishment. Life would now go back to normal.

Manfred watched their bodies go from white to a splendid orange, red to black peels, colours that flickered behind a thick curtain of dark smoke. There and then not.

# PART II

# CHAPTER 14

Anna wrung out the rag over the bucket, then knelt back down on the tavern floor. How dirty it always was now, always coated in dusty footprints. But no odious chore existed that could break Anna's overall good mood or wipe the smile from her lips for long. As she rinsed the floor, she let Manfred spin freely nearby with his spoon. It was very early in the morning, and none of the guests would be down for breakfast for at least another hour. She was slowly letting her firm grip on Manfred's peculiarities go. Who was she to declare what was odd in her son, when everyone else thought him so exceptional? She even worried she had been suppressing his extraordinariness with all her attempts at making him speak when he didn't wish to, or taking his spoon or his leaves or his stones or his song from him.

She had begun to laugh nervously at herself while she cleaned rooms, laundered sheets or stirred oats, watching

Manfred as he set up his collections again and again. How stupid she was, for ever thinking her son was enfeebled in any way. How stupid she was! It was laughable. She prayed more than ever, begging for forgiveness for her years of ignorance. At first she felt slightly estranged from God, for how could she only now see the message He had been sending her all along? How could she not see that it was His will that Manfred perfect song before ordinary language, because God would call upon Manfred and wanted him to be ready.

Was it not true, too, that all Manfred had ever suffered from was a short bout of dysentery and the snivels, never the measles or the long fevers Konrad had battled with? Was this not also a sign of God's protective embrace? Anna was fretful at the thought that she had attempted to shake God from her son and prayed incessantly for his forgiveness.

She looked up at the countless broadsheets nailed to the tavern wall, the many woodcut prints of Manfred, almost always with clouds hovering just above his head with doves bursting out from the clouds upon tides of sunshine. There were others of an even more epic variation, with Manfred's mouth blowing away the clouds with song. The city's three printers competed in quantity and sordidness and the seduction of Hans in the woods by his father, became comparatively more and more perverse, with Hans' father beckoning his son to kiss the anus of the devil.

Anna's favourite prints were the woodcuts that showed

the children being rescued from Herr and Frau Laumayer and Frau Zwenk, seven in total, holding vigil at Manfred's feet in gratitude. Not that this really happened, they weren't even at their parents' execution last month but, still, the sentiment was real. They were all orphans now. Upon their arrest both Herr Laumayer and Herr Zwenk accused their respective wives of being witches, claiming it was they who Hans' father had seen at the witches' sabbat. Only Herr Zwenk would be proven innocent after his wife admitted to having put mice dung in his food. She said the devil promised her the dung would remedy his gambling. Herr Zwenk had struggled with an illness shortly before his arrest and so was released from prison. He fled the day after, abandoning his children.

There was much discussion in the tavern afterwards on whether Herr Zwenk should have been released or not. Many believed his disappearance signified guilt, but these debates were eventually summed up: at least he was gone and the witch problem in the villages appeared to be over.

This was why Anna felt so free to indulge in studying this woodcut and her own presence in the illustration. She was depicted standing off to one side, looking, not at her son, but upwards in prayer, her shawl draped over her head, making her bear a close resemblance to a statue of Mary. A serene smile played on her lips (her lips much smaller in the woodcut). It wasn't a very good drawing really, there were far more talented engravers in on it now, but still she

147

marvelled at herself. She thought of the customers looking at it and then at her from across the room, and how they might feel admiration, even reverence. Never had she thought she would ever be painted – not that she was exactly painted there in the broadsheet, but it was her likeness. Who had the money for such things? How could she ever think of herself as so important to deserve reproduction, however crude.

In the ensuing month and a half after the first witch burnings, the Myrrh Tree tavern experienced a rush of new patrons. Anyone who could afford a single cup of wine tried to make their way to Wilhelm's tavern to drink it. The grape harvest went much better than expected, and though the price of wine had increased, it was not to such an exorbitant level as first predicted. It was estimated that less than one third of the vineyards had been harmed in the hail. The wine itself also suffered in quality, the subsequent rise in temperatures increased the alcohol level so much that it burned the mouth and the remaining aftertaste had a slightly musty quality, was as if some of the damaged grapes had made it into harvest. This hindered export to some degree; there were merchants who went to the next town, south of Flusstal, to buy a better quality wine. This kept the local prices at a more manageable level.

The drinking room was regularly crowded by late afternoon, with the hope of hearing Manfred sing though, now, a tavern song was never requested, just hymns. If Manfred had once been a draw to the tavern, he was now the main attraction. None of the rooms were ever vacant. The tavern had been bestowed with a new respectability that had far outreached its rundown appearance, though this too had slightly improved when a very pious and partially deaf glass-maker replaced the panel of the broken window in exchange for a good seat to hear Manfred better when he sang. The guild room had been opened up, and Wilhelm spoke about taking down the wall completely and setting up a small permanent platform for Manfred, and having just one large drinking room.

Many customers prayed in the tavern after Manfred was lowered off the empty wine cask he now stood upon to sing. It was such an odd sight, to see men kneeling down in front of the bench, resting their elbows where they once sat, eyes closed, a hovering sibilance.

This caused Wilhelm some discomfort but he no longer engaged in his old soliloquies of the tavern being the centre of a man's soul and so on. Instead he said the Lord's Prayer in place of a toast. Women and children joined their husbands now, this too was new for Wilhelm and sometimes he would stand in wonderment. 'Is this church or a tavern?' he would whisper to Margarethe, who would laugh a little more enthusiastically than the joke warranted.

But their takings increased, and this allowed the Myrrh Tree tavern to keep afloat. Anna was offered lower prices at the bakers and butchers. She needn't wait in line any more either, she was waved to the front.

This should have been enough to temper Wilhelm's appetite for wine, and it was true that he did not fall under the spell of drunkenness until much later in the day, usually after the more pious churching crowd had left and there remained in his tavern the heartier of the wine drinkers. For the first time, Wilhelm felt important and successful, but rather than leading him away from excess – an assumption of Anna's that this was all that was needed to make him stop – he seemed keen to indulge himself because of it. He rose on the tide of wine when joyful, sunk below it when miserable, but was always under its influence.

Anna would watch him as he downed cup after cup. All that had changed was the way he moved, the way his arms jutted out slightly from his sides so that he seemed to take up more space, the way he kept his knees spread further apart to seem larger. He sniffed more loudly and cleared his throat often, as if to draw glances from those he sat with, who assured him that his day had indeed arrived. He laughed less, as if to trade his once merry character for one more serious, until he had enough and was no longer careful enough to portray someone different. When he argued over backgammon or a card he had been dealt, when he verged on shattering his new facade of a man to contend with, Anna did not come to his aid. She knew this was not part of his new self-image of a man with a booming tavern and a son who returned the souls of witches to God.

In fact, the new demands of the tavern had left them rather distant from one another, and often they barely had a chance to eat supper together. Wilhelm would eat with the patrons and Anna would eat hurriedly, tucked away in the kitchen with Manfred, in order to temper the ever increasing demands for him to sing.

She rarely had a chance to sit down.

They did not discuss Manfred in any detail, but made simple comments on how well he sang, or relayed to one another how so and so had paid their son a wonderful compliment. It was as if they both feared that to speak too much about him would somehow undo the good fortune and prominence he had brought upon them and the tavern. It was as if their son was a house of cards and to prod at one single aspect of him could very well make the whole of him collapse.

Wilhelm had taken a new interest in him and rather than being filled with disgust when he finally caught Manfred lining up stones or spinning round with his spoon behind the tavern, rather than seeing it as pitiful as Anna once had, he felt only pride. He would just stand there, quietly watching, and Anna would have to fight an incredible urge to go and block Wilhelm's view or gather up Manfred's things. 'How mysterious he is,' Wilhelm would whisper, as if Manfred were sleeping, 'a genius.'

These were the moments in which he would look at her intensely, a glance filled with love and awe. Anna would have to say something to distract him, because the strength of it was too much, it forced her into a moment of reflection on Manfred, on her own mistakes with him. During these loving looks, Anna could also not help but feel an involuntary resentment towards Wilhelm. 'So now you are so interested in him? After all the pains I've taken to keep these peculiarities hidden, it was all so pointless because you never looked until now – and what would you have thought about your son before? Would you have loved him as you do now? As I always have.'

There was a sudden loud knock at the tavern door. Anna startled and approached it with much trepidation. Moments still existed when she was sure Manfred would be found out, and the buried anxiety of this would come over her in a jumble of nerves. However, Anna did not recognize this for what it was and, of late, considered herself oddly anxious.

She opened the door slowly, cautiously.

'Frau Wirth, my apologies for the early hour.' Father Gottlieb stood under the thin blue veins of morning light. He appeared quite pale. His usually neatly combed hair was mussed and sticking out at the back, making him look younger.

'Please come in, Father.' Anna motioned him inside. She had found a comfortable rapport with Father Gottlieb about Manfred in the last month. He would remind her that God is too infinite and complex for his flock to understand, and that there had been many faithful before Anna who had fumbled in their misconception of the subtleties of the Almighty.

With Father Gottlieb she found a perfect mixture of confession and absolution. She was reassured by his interest in her son. She no longer had to keep him hidden away. Her son was celebrated for his difference rather than abhorred. Sometimes, they could spend up to an hour discussing Manfred's brilliance. Brilliance was Father Gottlieb's word, and whenever he sensed Anna was becoming embarrassed by Manfred's uniqueness, he coaxed her along by reminding her that those who are in such close communication with God do not need to communicate with others in the usual way.

How clever their priest was, for did it not take genius to recognize genius?

Anna often wondered how she looked to the customers, conversing on higher matters as they sat there, curious as to what she and the priest were discussing.

Before or after these lengthy conversations, Gottlieb watched Manfred sing, often leading a prayer afterwards, or quoting scripture. 'Once this sinful city was like silver, once it was wine, but the sinful made the city worthless, turned wine into water. Let us be silver again, let us be wine in God's eye, by the grace of God let us expel those who think they live in the city of Sodom and not the decent Christian city of Flusstal.'

Anna led Father Gottlieb towards a table, 'Can I get you anything, Father?'

He ignored her question. 'I really must speak to your husband.'

Anna went into the kitchen and asked Margarethe to have Wilhelm come down.

When she returned, she saw Father Gottlieb looking at Manfred openly spinning with the spoon held above his head. How could she have forgotten? She'd become too relaxed. Anna descended on Manfred, reaching out to stop him, to strip him of his spoon, but Gottlieb stopped her.

'No, it's all right, please don't,' he said.

Anna paused, unsure what to do, feeling uneasy. 'I think he just likes the reflections in it, the shininess.' Then realizing the spoon was partially rusted. 'Or, well, the parts that are still bright. I should maybe try and shine it, or when the tinker is around . . .' she trailed off, feeling a sense of absurdity that she should talk so casually of her son who was spinning round and round with a spoon.

'For every one that doeth evil hateth the light, neither cometh to the light, lest his deeds should be reproved. But he that doeth truth cometh to the light, that his deeds may be made manifest, that they are wrought in God.' Gottlieb quoted from the Gospel of John, then made a short hum as if he now fully understood the passage, or maybe realized how fitting it was for Manfred.

They waited in an awkward silence, watching Manfred spin and jump until anyone else would have fallen over from dizziness. Finally he flopped down and focused on his unending task of arranging, which on that particular morning, was buttons that had been lost in the tavern. They did this until Wilhelm appeared, still tucking in his shirt, looking dishevelled, glassy eyed and reeking of wine.

'Good morning, Father.' Wilhelm tried to feign spryness, but his voice was too husky and low to make it believable he'd already been awake.

Wilhelm sat down next to Anna, facing Father Gottlieb.

'It is with a heavy heart,' the priest began, kissing the cross round his neck with his thin dry lips, before continuing, 'that I must report that the two youngest boys of Herr Laumayer and the youngest daughter of Herr Zwenk – she's just seven years old, in fact – are being plagued by the devil.' Father Gottlieb ran his hands over his face, leaving them resting on his cheeks a moment and, as a result, he drew the skin down round his eyes so they appeared slanted and showed a scattering of red blood vessels under his bottom lids. His neatly trimmed beard stuck out slightly between his fingers.

He sighed heavily, and for a moment Anna felt that the level of easy rapport she and Wilhelm had attained with Father Gottlieb was about to return, and they could shift away from this feeling of stiffness and discomfort.

'They've had to be isolated from the other children at the orphanage for fear the demonic influence that the devil has cast upon them will spread. They spent last night at the church. I saw it with my own eyes – the terror these children suffered, calling out all through the night that the devil was near. I would rush over and wake them, and they would fling themselves about. The devil is preying on their minds.'

They thought he was about to say more, but he did not. Anna could not help but feel mildly relieved – Manfred was still brilliant.

'Anything, Father, we can do to help. Please.'

Father Gottlieb sat up straighter, now he was a man of action, he flexed his hands into two heavy fists.

'I would like Manfred to come and sing to these children. Manfred would be a great comfort to them; his sublime singing would allow their souls to heal. They will also take comfort that he salvaged the souls of their parents. Could I take him in the evening, just after his supper? I could return him the next morning.'

'For just the one night, Father?'

'For as many nights as it takes.'

Wilhelm sat quietly for a moment. 'Is there any way you could bring the children here? Manfred sings here nearly each night.'

'These children, Herr Wirth, could not choose a new father or mother, they are not inviting the devil, and are only being visited by such evil because of who their parents

156

were. They haven't committed any crimes themselves, but the devil was promised their souls by their own mothers, and he wants them. This evil has infected them, and all I can do is pray for their souls and try to chase the devil out. I cannot very well exorcise demons here, your patrons would flee in terror,' he said this very quickly, urgently, as if he had little time to sit around and discuss what needed to be done. He shifted on the bench, glancing over at the tavern clock.

'It is just . . .' Wilhelm hummed as if unsure how to proceed. 'It is just that our patrons come to hear him sing; he is what fills our tavern.'

Anna felt herself shrinking down into the floor; he was hinting at being reimbursed. It was always about easy money with him, something that had always eluded him until now.

'Manfred is being called by a higher power than money just now.' Father Gottlieb's brown eyes widened helplessly, but his mouth tightened, his lips all but disappeared into his mouth as if he were holding back his next sentence which would surely be hostile if he did not receive the answer he wanted.

This odd divide in his long face, as if the top and bottom half were working independently of one another, made for a much more menacing appearance than if he had looked wholly frustrated. If this were meant to intimidate Wilhelm, it was effective.

'Yes, of course, Father, anything we can do, as my wife says, anything at all,' Wilhelm assented.

'But will my son be at risk of the devil's influence?' Anna asked, though she didn't really fear this (he would already be suffering), only that she felt it reflected poorly on her not to ask. She couldn't help but feel her usual pleasure at pleasing someone else, and a twitch went through her stomach at the thought that her favourite woodcut of Manfred would now be realized. She believed he'd only be away for a short time, a few nights at best.

'He is too much an instrument of God, Anna. If he were vulnerable, I would not risk him in the first place, but he would have been affected already by the witches we visited in prison. He's immune.' He looked sympathetic and gave a sad smile. 'I will see you this evening then.'

Before he left, Anna and Father Gottlieb stood by the door, quickly discussing what Manfred would need to pack to spend the night at the church. He assured her again that Manfred was not at all at risk.

'Think of it, Anna, your son is helping fight the most epic battle waged in the heart of every man, and he's winning, Anna, he's winning!'

And as she packed Manfred some cheese and various dried fruits – the foods he ate with the least amount of sulkiness, she repeated Father Gottlieb's words in her mind over and over, in a kind of frenzied giddiness. She knew she should have felt more remorse for the stricken children. But she had done what she could by offering the aid of her son. Once the children were healed, saved, they would live to talk about Manfred's impact upon them and this would follow him for the rest of his life.

His genius would be secured then, his legacy of goodness.

Partly because of her mood and because Father Gottlieb reacted as he did and partly because she wanted Manfred to be comforted if he were to become homesick, at the last minute, Anna packed his spoon.

# CHAPTER 15

With a candle so near her face, the sleeping girl's eyelids appeared to be various shades of pink as they rippled on the exterior from the pressure of her flickering eyes. Manfred noticed this, but only briefly. It could hardly hold his attention for long while inside the church in the midst of the glorious collection of colour that was rising all round him as the light of dawn came in through the stained-glass windows.

At dawn it could not be helped that Manfred sang his last song almost absentmindedly, but his voice was at its height of beauty and emerged from his mouth as a serpentine ribbon that rode the incoming light as easily as sunlight does on the surface of the Neckar river. It brought warmth and comfort to the children who were only now able finally to sleep. Manfred's duty was to soothe the children before and after Father Gottlieb led them in prayer, doused them with holy water and consecrated salt and demanded that the evil that pained them so, vacate.

In between, he was allowed to do as he wished. He stood by the votive offerings at the shrine of Mary which were kept lit through the night, a symphonic whole he could sway to. He rolled under the pews with the small toys Father Gottlieb made available for all the children. He took all the small carvings of wooden horses and lined them up, one by one, in tidy pursuit of orderliness. He slept when he wanted, and Father Gottlieb used Manfred's sound sleeping as an example of what the children could hope to achieve one night. Manfred would only be woken again, if any of the children fell asleep accidentally. Father would shake the child awake, not right away, however. He believed it was all about timing. If too soon, they would see nothing, if too late, their souls would be in jeopardy of being devoured and they would wake unchristian. Then he sat quietly with them, comforting them, asking exactly what they had seen.

The line between dream and wakefulness was blurred in the first moments after the cold holy water jolted them into consciousness. There, in the ethereal setting of the church with its soaring ceiling, under the influence of Manfred's songs and with Father Gottlieb's stricken face hovering above them with a look of desperate expectation, they would tell their dreams. Or better, variations of the same dream.

Upon falling asleep, they would feel themselves being lifted upwards. They could see their own bodies left behind, curled up on the pew tucked into the wool blankets, but they'd appear lumpy like discarded sacks of potatoes. They'd float above the candles, above Father Gottlieb and the altar where the Eucharist is administered, and then suddenly they were outside the church. At this point they would see they were riding on one of the pews. Finally they would be set down at the witches' sabbat, held, they believed, in the woods near to their village. They were chased at this point, by a dog with lips that curled back into a demonic hungry sneer, by strange sounds, by witches who paused in their frenetic dances – they knew these witches were plotting to eat them – and by shadowy figures that had yet to take full shape.

Faces were mostly obscured by the darkness and, because they were being chased, the children faced away from their pursuers, but they did see other children there, who were being chased as well. In the first week Herr Zwenk's daughter claimed to have seen her good friend, and the son of Herr Laumayer saw his cousin.

The church went from housing three children to fifteen. Six more children came in from the villages. The first child within the city walls to be spotted at the witches' sabbat was an eight-year-old altar boy from Father Gottlieb's own church. This deepened the panic in the city, for the storm on the horizon now hovered above them. The altar boy would soon see his stepbrother, and in turn his stepbrother would see another boy whom he abhorred and was not all surprised to see there and, who in his opinion, was enjoying very much the odd meat he was eating in the dream. The boy whom he abhorred would see his younger sister and a neighbour's son. The neighbour's son, a bricklayer's apprentice, dreamt of his master's son soon after his arrival.

It was a fortnight before Herr Zwenk's daughter was finally caught and dragged by one ankle towards a towering bonfire. Masked faces – the masks themselves were bone white and without any decoration – flickered in and out of the shadows. She caught glimpses of pointed teeth and long forked tongues. She kicked and kicked with her other leg and tried to get away, but her captor caught both legs and there was nothing she could do; she could feel the fire lapping at her toes. This was when she managed to turn and see it was her father who had her legs. Father Gottlieb had believed all along in Herr Zwenk's guilt and this was confirmation. Oh, how Father Gottlieb would dote on Herr Zwenk's daughter in the days after she revealed this to him, no refill was denied, no cake was too many. Herr Zwenk's daughter ate better than in all her previous seven years.

Manfred was unmindful of all this. He knew once he finished singing to this girl, whose eyelids had finally relaxed, he would again have his spoon. He would be able to spin freely up and down the aisle, spoon in hand, attempting to capture various reflections of candlelight in the spoon's hollow so that it could be gathered there in some spectacular luminous whole. Manfred felt the spoon before he took it in visually. He felt the weight of it pushing into his hand, and he went taut with anticipation. He heard someone speaking, but it was incomprehensible, just a meaningless percussion.

He didn't notice how Father Gottlieb stood beside him watching with fascination. Manfred felt a hand over his own, dry and cool, smooth as well, trying to press his hand closed on the unfamiliar object resting in his palm. It was not his spoon but Manfred gripped it.

It was then he looked down at his hand, at what was being forced inside it. The thing blazed in his palm, it was a glorious sight, stunning and perfect. How could such loveliness be reduced to something hand-held? It was a golden spoon and etched into its handle was an image of Jesus hanging from the cross. Manfred was only interested in the elongated oval shape of the bowl of the spoon. It was larger than the one he had with him, and in its hollow the church light was reflected but with gold gauzily transposed over it.

Father Gottlieb chuckled, pleased that his young prodigy was so delighted by his gift. If he had knelt down in that moment in front of Manfred when he closed his hand on his gift, he would have likely felt the spoon against his own cheeks as a gesture of affection and simple curiosity. Putting a spoon against another's cheek, pressing down just so, so that the excess of cheek bulged up round the spoon's hollow brought Manfred a mysterious glee. What Gottlieb did do, however, was rest his hand between Manfred's shoulders, feeling the delicacy of his two shoulderblades under his thin linen shirt that seemed to retain the incoming sun's heat, adding to the confounding sensation that travelled up through Gottlieb's arm to his heart. He likened it to how a bird would feel just between its wings as it soared high in the sky. A seraph, right there under his hands. Oh, the heat he felt emanate off Manfred's back, was like nothing else he had ever felt. The subtle rise and fall of his slight shoulders seemed proof of the gentlest life inside him. The beauty of this child's face, the threads of gold through his flaxen hair seemed to writhe in the sun as if through its follicles burst fine brilliant filaments. Even the way the light passed through his ears, the faintest pinkish-red vessels so vibrant in those delicate whorls, affirmed the godliness of this child. Gottlieb thought it no coincidence that Manfred had sung on his church steps. He knew he was being asked by God for something. He had waited all his life for this, to be called upon.

Once Gottlieb's hand retreated, Manfred stood still a moment, his free hand clenched into a fist, his eyes squinting into the spoon with excitement. Perhaps because Herr Zwenk's daughter was so close to him, and because he was so thrilled with his new gift and the endless possibilities it provided in capturing the sublime beauty of light, he pressed the spoon to her face.

She woke with a start. Looking up she must have seen the shadow of Manfred's face and the way the light caught the top of his head. In combination with her sleepiness it must have seemed like a halo. This only affirmed what she always wanted to believe about Manfred, what everyone already said about him, that he was angelic. Though she personally had her doubts whether Manfred was anything special except for his pretty singing voice, because of her grief over being abandoned by her father, for her dead mother, and thinking that God must have deserted her or why else should she have been the recipient of so much loss, she believed in Manfred then. For Jesus was right there in the periphery of her vision, blurred because of the closeness of the spoon. God had returned and Manfred had brought him.

She reached up and caressed the spoon, and held it in place against her cheek.

Herr Zwenk's daughter would have no more bad dreams. She would always claim that through Manfred's spoon arrived the power of Jesus, which healed her of her parent's transgressions and freed her from the nightly pursuit of witches.

It was Manfred's spoon, she would say until the end of her days, that saved her.

# CHAPTER 16

On the third Sunday that Holy Cross church housed the sleep-deprived children it was bestowed the nickname the 'wake-house'. Each week more and more children were sent there. Anna was sure it was someone in her tavern who had been the first to utter it and from there it seemed to catch on. But on Sunday, it was again just church. Anna was settled in for Mass, wondering whether or not any of the children slept on the pew she was sitting upon. She tried to picture the somnolent children scattered throughout the church, sleeping here and there, leaning against the statue of Mary or the base of altar.

She wondered where Manfred slept, on which pew. And she allowed herself to think that he likely slept on the pew where she always sat, as if he could sniff her out like a pup for his mother. This image suddenly disgusted her and she pushed it quickly from her mind.

Manfred was rarely returned to the tavern and Anna missed him terribly. Manfred, because he was not personally plagued by witches, was still supposed to come home during the day. This was the intended arrangement. At first Father Gottlieb explained that sometimes he would fall asleep in the church, and rather than disturb him he would just let him be. And, he said, when Manfred woke, it was usually too late to take him back to the tavern and in this spare time he thought it would best benefit their son to teach him to sign his name and write his letters.

'In fact,' Father Gottlieb said, 'his enthusiasm for learning letters, well, I've never seen the like before. He's just so astute. It is quite amazing how quickly he's caught on; it's just a matter of time before we can move on to reading.'

It was true that when the other children slept into the afternoons, Father Gottlieb would write out the alphabet, and Manfred would trace over each letter with his finger. He did it over and over and within days he could write it out himself from memory. 'A', he would write, then he would sing it, his lilting voice arching over the 'Aaaaaaa, Beeeeeee,' and gradually tapering off gently.

Manfred would ask for the letter A or B, and Father Gottlieb would quickly provide him with chalk and slate. Manfred could sit for over an hour writing and rewriting the alphabet, taking particular care for his favourite letters, which were M, P and K just then.

Anna tested it herself, giving Manfred a bit of paper and

168

an inked quill, and slowly, with the care Father Gottlieb had described, he filled the paper with several Ms and Ks, squeezing in small vertical Ps as he rotated the paper, as if they were a series of patched eyes around the paper's edges. His penmanship had the artistry of a practised scribe.

Despite the horrors that afflicted other children, Anna would always look back on this period as one of personal contentment and, when she was ready, one of grave ignorance. For Manfred treated letters just as he treated his other collections: he lined them up in order and just as often not in order so that he could again list them in order. He liked whatever he alone saw in them, not because letters were the seedlings of language, but entities to be arranged and rearranged, objects he did not have to go out searching for but which were right there at the ends of his fingertips whenever he so chose to conjure them.

But at the time Anna thought none of this, and only saw her son progressing intellectually under the influence of the priest, and progressing spiritually all those round him.

Her long-running worry for her son had finally been lifted, and oh, how different her life was in his absence. She could again linger at the water pump, and invite her neighbours into the kitchen where it was warmer to continue their conversations. She milled about longer in the market, basking in the recent attention Manfred's singing had brought her. She'd be elated over the increasing frequency that vendors, through sleight of hand, lowered their prices just for her. There was a steady stream of gifts being brought to the tavern, food mostly: fresh loaves of bread with new churned butter, fried cakes, fish, cheese. So much food that at times Anna had to serve it to her guests and so reaped all the profit. But most importantly, much to Wilhelm's delight, the weaver's guild was enquiring about using the tavern as their official meeting place.

So because Anna was seeing Manfred less and less, she looked forward to Sunday morning Mass, because she could bring him back to the tavern with her once the service was finished and the tavern was overflowing with patrons. And, she didn't worry about him any more. This isn't to say she wasn't saddened by his absence, but she thought it was much the same as if he were sent off to school at St Benedict's monastery, which only the sons of nobles and wealthy merchants attended. This would fill her with giddiness, so much so, she lost sight at times of where her son really was, and what his real purpose there was. She tended to only think of him as thriving.

The church service continued in the same vein, passages from Leviticus were read and the evils of sodomy were expounded. Father Gottlieb also read from Leviticus the endorsements of quarantine for those infected with disease and said that the children were spiritually diseased and applauded those who had already had the astuteness to recognize this truth and bring them to the wake-house.

The only difference was that the children who stayed at

the wake-house sat in the first row of pews, rather than with their own families. There were now four children from the city staying in the wake-house. They glanced back from time to time, both to seek out their friends and family, and also because they were filled with self-importance being up front, and wanted see if anyone was looking at them, turning back round quickly, satisfied that they were.

Anna tried to work out who was who, and exactly what she had heard about each from the plethora of information on the broadsheets posted in the tavern.

Another difference was that a collection plate went up and down the pews. 'For the wake-house, for the suffering children, who need blankets and food and wood, give of yourself to keep the children safe and in turn you protect your own. Witches will not thrive in Flusstal as they do elsewhere, it will not happen here,' Father Gottlieb instructed them. Everyone turned round and back and round again, to watch what others placed in the plate. If it was too little they would be given an accusatory scowl. Later, as the gossip spread round quickly and hot whispers filled the church, no one would speak to the man or his wife on the church steps. Worse, it might be suggested that perhaps there was a darker reason why they did not want to donate – those who withheld their charity were witches.

Manfred sat closest to the aisle in the first centre pew, slightly swinging his legs, his attention as usual on the stained-glass windows.

The reason for this new seating arrangement soon became obvious when Father Gottlieb called upon one child to give 'testimony' to their own nightly abduction. Herr Zwenk's daughter went first, but her voice was too timid and she broke down and cried, so Father Gottlieb continued for her. He re-told what Herr Zwenk's daughter witnessed in her dreams, sparing no detail, managing to convey her relentless and savage pursuit by the witches. They came at her, he said, running on all fours like animals, creatures of the night, leaping and bounding through the forest to open meadows that glowed with white clover under the moonlight. Soon it felt as if the whole congregation were with Herr Zwenk's daughter being chased as well. When the witches stood up, their legs and arms were thin and long, their hands had fingers that jutted out like spindly claws, their faces were featureless. Except Herr Zwenk's daughter could now say for sure that one was her father.

And what would Herr Zwenk do once he caught his daughter? There was something incestuous intimated, a sense that her own father planned to devour her somehow, alter her purity just as Hans' father had by sending his son to be sodomized by the devil.

It would only be upon later reflection, Anna would think that the evil witches Father Gottlieb had described sounded like a child's stick-man scrawl.

'Children obey their fathers up until the point their fathers stop obeying God. If a child's father has gone to the devil, then that child can no longer obey his father or mother without also turning against God. But a child is a fool, as it says in Proverbs. Foolishness is bound up in a child's heart and he will often follow his parents down the dark path to hell rather than go to God. But are these children responsible? We do not execute fools and so we do not execute children. So these children here before us, who are now being attacked during the night, being accosted by witches, tempted by cakes and baubles, must be salvaged, the wreckage of their souls healed and returned to God.

'But the *miracle* is – the *miracle* is.' Father Gottlieb, now into his easy style of speaking, repeated himself, putting emphasis on miracle so that its last syllable cut like a scythe – 'Herr Zwenk's daughter has defeated the witches.' He paused, so that the stirring of his audience could be heard, and this added to the building eagerness to hear how this slight girl with untidy hair had fought off witches.

'She is able to go back to her village and live with her aunt. Dreams no longer plague her. She is free from witches, free to live her life as she wants, as a good Catholic. Why? you wonder. Why is this girl saved? Because God has given us, this city, this parish, you and I, a weapon to fight the devil's brethren. Our Lord almighty has blessed us with a means to have his children restored to good faith, to break their parent's promise of their souls to the devil.'

Father Gottlieb stepped forward and lifted Manfred up from the pew to the bottom step leading up to the altar.

How small he looked in his white altar-boy robe, how tidy he looked with his hair neatly combed. Once set down, Manfred seemed somewhat stunned, and looked as if he wanted to go back to where he had been sitting, but then Gottlieb gently rested his hand on Manfred's shoulder, bent down and began to sing into his ear, steering him towards the hymn he wished Manfred to sing, turning him towards the windows.

Then Manfred's voice rose softly into the air and everyone went still and strained to hear him:

> 'O, sisters, too, how may we do,
> For to preserve this day.
> This poor youngling for whom we do sing
> Bye, bye, lully, lullay.
>
> Herod, the king, in his raging,
> Charged he hath this day
> His men of might, in his own sight,
> All children young to slay.
>
> That woe is me, poor child for thee!
> And every mourn and day,
> For thy parting neither say nor sing,
> Bye, bye, lully, lullay.

The significance of the song was lost on no one. Based

on the massacre of the innocents in the Gospel of Matthew, it was a mother's lament for her infant son condemned to die under Herod's despicable order. Herod, the pagan king, wanted to kill the infant Jesus but couldn't find him and so commanded that all male infants in his kingdom be killed, in the hope that Jesus would be one of them.

Herod was interchangeable with witch. The witches wanted their infants dead. They wanted their sons, and their daughters too. They wanted desiccation of wombs, of crops, they wanted the earth to be a desert of misery.

The women began to weep, rosary beads wove through their fingers like knotted black snakes, Manfred returned to the beginning and sang the song all the way through again. His small, solo voice was like a beating heart, it was life itself. As he sang Father Gottlieb's voice rose as he spoke over him. It came down over his flock like a hand reaching out to the drowning. 'I wish to share with you the miracle of this child. Many have come to me and asked if it was true and now I answer, yes. As God showed himself in the form of an angel to the shepherds on the eve of our Saviour's birth, and told them not to be afraid, that he was bringing them good news of great joy for all the people – the people of those days and the people of today – and Jesus, our Saviour, the promised Messiah, was born so this child, too, brings good news, that wickedness will not win over good, that the battle between evil and good fought each day in the shadows round us will be flooded with light and exposed.

'This child, is the shepherd of this light. Already he has proved this with his singing praise of God which banished the rain clouds from our skies and returned the sun. Already he has shown that as he sings to witches he can loosen Satan's grip from their souls. God has granted us a healer.'

Anna smiled, and looked into her lap demurely, hoping to give the appearance of a proud mother but not boastful. She glanced quickly at the statue of St Mary and tried to mimic the softness round her eyes, the pained look, and so missed that Father Gottlieb had turned around to get something.

When she finally looked up again, the demure, pained look fell from her face.

Father Gottlieb had given Manfred a spoon.

Manfred peered into its hollow, then turned it once, twice, as if it really were a compass and he was trying to find the direction necessary to travel towards God. He bent his legs, then jumped straight up, his free hand flapping at his side. Finally he began to spin, the spoon inches from his nose.

Anna moved to the edge of the pew. She heard Konrad mutter something unintelligible beside her. She waited for some kind of indictment of Manfred or her. She felt betrayed that Father Gottlieb would reveal publicly what she considered private, even if she now equated her son's affection for a spoon to a mere facial tic, a stutter at worst.

How could he humiliate her son like this?

'Just as witches have been known to use everyday kitchen items to incite their evil-doings – brooms to fly off to their dances, pots to stir up storms – well, God, too, is in the kitchen. It is in this spoon that God has shown himself to this child.' Father Gottlieb knelt down near Manfred, and began to pray.

Details weren't required just then, no one needed to know exactly how the spoon worked. This information would quickly become available in an even greater onslaught of broadsheets and woodcuts, where various renditions of Jesus' face flickered in the spoon only for Manfred's eyes.

Just as it was at the tavern, at the burning of Hans, the whole congregation fell to their knees, palms raised above their heads in prayer.

Those in church who attended Sunday Mass only because it was expected of them and so their regular presence was habitual in order to fulfil their civic duty, rather than spiritual, were not filled with scepticism as one would suspect. Instead, these churchgoers felt relieved of the doubt they had begun to experience after the rapture over Manfred's first miracle on the church steps had worn off. They had entertained thoughts on coincidence, maybe the sky had been about to clear anyway. But now, the aesthetic appeal of this same golden boy spinning in the house of the Lord, with a golden spoon in his grasp, like a weathervane turning on the winds of heaven, proved too moving to doubt that this child was touched by God. So even the sceptics found themselves relinquishing their doubts.

God reaching out directly to the people of Flusstal was too nice a thought to resist.

# CHAPTER 17

Manfred was the only thing the other children could talk about behind the church. He was, after all, one of them, or better, they had once been his age so he was an object of fascination because he had accomplished something extraordinary; he had gained the undivided attention and good opinion of all the adults round them. They had started to emulate Manfred, or better what they believed Manfred was like at home – soft spoken and compliant, he tired at the right time and woke easily in the morning – for as long as they could keep it up, which usually didn't amount to a great ddeal of time. It proved difficult to always be so good. Some had even taken to singing more, hoping someone walking by would notice, and compliment them, hoping even more secretly that they too possessed a voice that could change the weather, or at the very least bring them recognition. This was followed by a jealous frustration when they realized they were not special. Second best was to know Manfred or anyone associated with him, better than their companions did. They wanted any kind of knowledge that would allow them to smugly state things like: 'Manfred is like this, his dislikes are this and that, he's not interested in toys . . .'

Today, they would likely go home and spend the rest of the day staring into spoons.

At least this was how Konrad felt after standing behind the church for just a few moments on that Spoon Sunday, as he would always internally call it.

'Hey, hey!'

Everyone flocked round him. It was still cool, frost had coated the grass that morning and time behind the church would become more limited as the weather turned colder. Konrad pretended to be above the maelstrom gathering round him. He nodded to the compliments he was forced to accept on Manfred's behalf. 'He made my mother cry', 'Tell him that I prayed for him', 'He's so sweet . . . precious', 'Have him ask God to bless me', 'I dreamt of him.' He ignored the three blonde daughters of Erhard and Rebekka standing in a small circle, singing 'The Massacre of the Innocents', over and over, harmonizing with the youngest who was attempting Manfred's lilting pitch.

Really he felt as if he were about to cry, shout insults, such was his feeling of overwhelming frustration. They were all so convinced by Manfred. Konrad had no idea he feared falling into obscurity next to the rising fame of his brother, instead he only wanted the truth about his brother to be known – that he was ordinary in every way, and extraordinary only in deceit. Yet, his loyalty to his mother prevented him from revealing this truth. It did help that Konrad was enjoying a new popularity.

On previous Sundays behind the church, though Manfred was often brought up, the conversations had mostly focused on witches, with Konrad offering up his many versions of witches storming the wine cellar. Since describing Hans' invasion, there had been other, even more threatening attempts at burglarizing wine by witches, and his listeners remained riveted, mulling over these new developments in Konrad's narrative. Slowly they would respond with their own personal encounters with witches, but they never interrupted him. Though games were no longer played much, Konrad suspected that once they did resume, he would be included in any and all of them and would never again be thought of as an annoyance.

Everyone tended to stay together in one group excitedly discussing witches, no longer breaking into their small factions. The girls no longer separated themselves into small clusters away from the boys. One six-year-old boy had said Ruprecht, St Niklaus' nefarious helper, had shown up under his bed recently and spent the night poking a rod into his mattress, singing that come St Niklaus' day, Ruprecht would put the boy in his sack and take him away to the Black Forest for being naughty. He also wanted the boy to perform songs at all hours of the night, and so the boy could do nothing but hum away until he was allowed to fall asleep, much to the annoyance of his siblings also sleeping in the room.

'But I've never been naughty,' the boy claimed defensively, shaking his head at the injustice. Konrad suspected that perhaps this particular boy was just overly anticipating the Christmas season, which was still a month away. Even when the older children told him Ruprecht didn't exist, the boy was still insistent he did, and was under his bed more times than he could count.

Another child, Juliane, said she saw a duck turn into a man with a black feathered face by the river, where everyone knew her mother made her carry her sheets to wash them in the river, so as to humiliate her into not wetting the bed any more.

There was a sense of forced bravado among the older boys, a tendency to approach the fearsome subject of witches with attempts to be funny to cover their fear.

Last Sunday, one of the first things Friedrich said was, 'How does a man scream rape when the devil is sodomizing him?' He then lifted one leg and let out a long fart. The stench mingled with groans of disgust and dizzying laughter. This made Friedrich laugh even harder. Some of the girls nearby scattered, though not for long.

Konrad knew this wasn't an original joke, he had heard it twice now in the tavern stable and considered pointing this out. Then he thought maybe he had heard it from Friedrich's father, and this somehow made it all right that Friedrich was saying it now.

This was how the talk of witches and the devil began among the older boys – light-heartedly – but soon they began swapping stories of witch sightings and things they had heard or seen in the circulating woodcuts.

Both boys and girls shared equally their fascination with the woodcuts. They were an education about the opposite sex, one's own sex and copulation. From the woodcuts one could gather what was wrong, what not to do, what feelings or ideas were perverse and shameful. The broadsheets were everywhere and showed orgiastic depictions of men kissing the devil's anus, women washing themselves in contorted positions, their hands lost some place between their legs, of women straddling goats, bare breasted, their uncovered heads wildly flung back in pleasure. Grotesque but intriguing.

And while the youngest children feared being eaten by witches, the older ones en route to maturity, feared something altogether different and could not help but constantly fix on that which was repeatedly said to be wicked: lust. It was necessary to ensure that you felt nothing, no sort of tingling, when viewing these images. If you did, then you were open to the devil, asking for it, calling upon witches.

The talk was a sort of effort at self-reassurance – that what one felt was repulsion and not arousal. Yet to Konrad, the whole conversation was about the sex act. Like pulling a string of snot out from one's nose, each tried to be more gross than the other; the grosser the better; the grosser the more repulsive and yet oddly the more enticing. 'Witches get poop in their mouths from kissing the devil's anus,' someone might say, and laughter would follow, but the image of lips on shameful parts was accompanied by a strange excited flutter and then terror for having felt it.

A terror that would not be moderated by bravado or humour once they were in their beds at night in the quiet.

This subject was tempered with much discussion about the children who sat on the front pews and who did not come outside, but went into the back of the church after the service. This left those behind the church speculating what it was they did there. Some thought some kind of banquet was served, or they had toys or goodies, some thought they just slept. They were so mysterious, these children, even those they had known since birth, their friends and cousins, who were now staying in the wake-house, had become enigmas. Mostly, it was believed, they had full access to Manfred which they all envied. This contact would surely bring out their better nature and, as a result, bring them more attention.

On the way to the tavern, Konrad and Caspar walked slowly, trying not to arrive too quickly back at their daily chores.

'It's so extraordinary, isn't it? How God has shown

184

himself to Manfred,' Caspar said suddenly. They had never before held much of a discussion on Manfred, not that Caspar hadn't attempted this before, just always with a more roundabout approach. Konrad usually deflected his attempts by quickly changing the subject, or saying he was in a hurry and jogging off. He could see now, though, that Caspar was also enjoying the attention being extended to him because of living with Manfred. Now that he thought more about it, Caspar was always entertaining a smaller group of servant boys behind the church, likely with his own stories. Konrad worried he may have contradicted his own witch stories. He suddenly realized he felt quite territorial, that this attention should only be his, considering how much effort he had put into his brother.

'I've known about it for a long while.'

'What? You did!?' Caspar jumped in front of him.

'Oh yes.'

'When did you find out? How long have you known?'

Konrad hadn't expected to be questioned further.

'I really can't remember when I first realized it.' He brushed by Caspar, forcing him to turn round and walk next to him, but he could feel Caspar peering at him sideways and knew he didn't believe him.

'Oh. I guessed you would have known,' Caspar said dismissively.

Konrad knew he sounded too vague to be convincing.

185

'I damn well did!' Konrad said, quite loudly. The taste of swearing lingered sweetly on his tongue. Then a moment later, he said in a more rational, conspiratorial voice, 'I had to keep it quiet.'

'But why?' Caspar demanded. His round eyes blinked quickly, his cheeks were pink from the cool air and from walking so briskly.

For a moment Konrad almost wished he was Caspar, living so much of his life underneath the tavern, at the periphery of those who lived above and at an emotional distance so he felt nothing more than a tepid affection towards them.

Konrad shook his head, closed and opened his eyes really slowly, as if he could hardly bear Caspar's impertinence, then he said very calmly, 'Shut up. I don't really need to tell you anything.'

Caspar slowed down and trailed behind him, and Konrad sped up into a sulky march. He went over what he could say in his mind to make himself sound more believable. He stopped and waited for Caspar to catch up to him.

'Listen, anyone in my brother's position – well, there is always a chance people will just think he's mad and this was something I didn't want to risk. So I prayed, very much, and because of my prayers I just knew that when the time was right, when it was safe enough, Manfred's ability would be revealed. God chose the right time.' Konrad felt dis-

186

gusted with himself that he was furthering the lie about Manfred and yet, he was quite impressed and satisfied that he was able to implicate himself in the process of his brother's rise to fame.

Caspar only nodded.

Konrad spent the next hour filling the water troughs for the ever increasing number of horses stabled at their tavern. It seemed all he did was fill and refill the troughs, pitch hay for gluttonous horses, then shovel the never ending piles of shit into barrels to be sold as fertilizer.

He always took pleasure in turning someone away, telling them that the stable was full, and there was nowhere left to tether their horse outside either. They would just stable their horses at some nearby place, and walk over, but at least he didn't need to tend them.

Eventually, looking for something to eat, Konrad skulked about in the kitchen. He watched scornfully how his mother flitted around in a state of busyness, inebriated by all the attention she was receiving.

Why is it, he wanted to march right up to his mother in front of everyone and ask, why is it that Manfred's been playing with a damned spoon for how long and now it is suddenly illuminated with God while here at home you were too embarrassed to let him have it most of the time? And now it's as if you are taking credit for it. His heartbeat sped up, and he really felt as if he were about to go over to his mother and say all his angry thoughts out loud. But he knew he wouldn't.

Instead he just listened for a short while, as he sat on a stool near the back door and ate some meat pie brought over by someone from church. It was very good. He savoured the thick cuts of pork inside a light buttery crust. Perhaps the best meat pie he'd ever eaten.

He listened as two women, whom he didn't recognize at all, stirred something in a pot while the other cut up beets next to her, her fingers stained red.

'It's the gambling that the devil gets you with,' one said. 'A man starts praying to fortune and not Jesus, and there it is – he's got the devil nipping at his heels.'

'And tobacco, mark my words,' said the other. 'Ever since it's been brought over here from those heathen lands, there's been more trouble.'

They were whispering, in fact the whole kitchen was whispering because Manfred was upstairs asleep and care was taken by all not to wake him. Even as they clanked pots and pans, as they heated up stews and meat pies and bread, they instinctively muttered apologies or cringed at themselves. Konrad hated it when Manfred was at home. When he wasn't there Konrad felt free of that nagging bite in his gut and head, and just utter relief from not having to hear his brother sing.

His mood lifted however when he saw Juditha's stepmother enter from the drinking room, having just arrived.

Finally, he thought. This would mean Juditha was very likely in the stable. He put his plate with his half-eaten meat pie on the table and went to see.

Sure enough she was there, still in her Sunday dress, feeding one of the horses. He was not surprised, it had become almost natural now to see her there. She was always so unaccounted for; she could always go missing and never be looked for.

'Aren't you worried you'll get it dirty?' He gestured to her dress, which was like her other one, too small and barely grazing her ankles.

She shook her head. 'When I get a new one, I will take better care of it.'

They fell into their usual awkward silence. They knew what they were both waiting for, but it was always prefaced with this clumsiness of where and when to begin. It was always at this point that Konrad acted most annoyed by her presence, but this time more so, because he was impatient to begin their game.

'I already fed that one,' he snapped.

She asked him if he'd seen some boy jump off the top step of the church when his mother wasn't looking and Konrad replied that no, he must have left before that happened.

'He looked like he was flying, for a second.'

This mention of flying, seemed invitation enough.

'Eat this,' Konrad directed her, his empty hand open before her nose.

'What is it?' her voice was filled with awe, the game had begun. She looked at him, back to his hand, back and forth.

'Tobacco.'

Juditha feigned protest; this too was part of the game. Konrad threw the imaginary contents of his hand at her and she pretended to go slack, now under the influence of some potion, today tobacco.

Then they heard a customer arrive. Juditha quickly ran and hid by the saddle racks, while Konrad went to tell him that the stable was full.

He returned, but because the spell was broken, both in their game and between them, they returned to their previous awkwardness, but at least it was brief.

Konrad fed her the imaginary tobacco and again she quickly pretended to be enchanted. He began to tie her wrists, then more meticulously he started to tie her arms against her sides with an invisible rope, deliberately brushing his hands against her small, pointy breasts. Then he started on her legs and ankles, trying to glimpse up her skirt. She never complained. She was quite pliable in these situations, completely in the character of someone one who had been bewitched. Konrad took full advantage. He noticed she had hair. It poked out from where her undergarments had worn thin, dark sprigs like the fur of some sleeping animal. She had much more than he did, and this annoyed him. At times he wanted to tease her about being a hairy girl, but then she would know he could see it, and might prevent him from seeing it again.

Once she was fully under his command – this was his favourite part – they pretended to be at the witches' sabbat and here was when the game would gradually go downhill. Juditha would frequently break from character by telling him what to do next, reminding him this or that wasn't quite right, or what foods were served at the banquet, down to the sauces, relishes and sweets, and how undercooked the meat was, which was really infant flesh, as if by saying these details out loud brought the scene to life. These interruptions were tedious for Konrad, and he only endured them for those other fruitful moments, when he had to handle Juditha again and bring her before Satan. She always did her best to squirm away from him, and he could brush against her and get a feel of what a girl's body was like.

They would sometimes quarrel, for example when Konrad picked up a handful of hay and dropped it over her head, saying it was unholy water and she became angry, not because he tossed hay over her but because it wasn't authentic enough. It didn't seem real enough. 'It would have been better to just make a sprinkling motion!' she complained as she brushed herself off. There was also the time when he started laughing, in what he thought sounded like a witch's cackle, but she insisted it just sounded stupid and ruined the mood of things and that he should try to do it with a more sinister tone. Konrad would then refuse to play any more. 'This is silly,' he would suddenly exclaim, extracting himself completely from the invention and putting the blame solely on Juditha for ever wanting to play 'witch's dance' anyway.

When Juditha first started hanging round the stable, she usually wanted to play Mary giving birth to baby Jesus. He went along for the same reasons he did now; he could see up her skirt as he played Joseph waiting to catch the Son of God. Once she wanted to pretend she was giving birth to Manfred, but Konrad refused to have anything to do with that, and demanded she never mention his brother again. She had started loitering by the stable for his attention before Manfred had first sung on the church steps, and the attention she proffered was Konrad's alone.

This time he skipped all the feasts, witchery and flying. 'Kiss my bum, kiss my bum,' he demanded, in what even he recognized as obnoxious chiding. He really wasn't in the mood for more pretence and wanted only to push for that part of the game he enjoyed without having to go through any of the effort.

He turned round and pointed his behind towards Juditha, who pushed him away with a half-hearted, 'Ew.' This urged him on. Her apparent repulsion made it funny, and he liked this sudden reversal of him controlling the game.

'But you must, I am your master.' He lowered his voice,

now in the full character of a seductive witch. Never did he call himself witch or devil, that would be going too far, even for him.

'As you wish, master,' she said and passively kissed him over his breeches.

This surprised Konrad, never had she kissed him before, never had he before thought to get her to do so. He wasn't sure if he could even kiss her on the lips, and here she was kissing him on the bum. Curious to see how far he could push her, Konrad brazenly pulled his breeches down slightly, his shirt falling loose and she kissed him again on his exposed buttocks, this time she made feigned sobbing noises. He turned towards her, keeping his now erect penis hidden under this shirt.

'Now lie down.'

Again, she did as she was told, choosing the tidiest spot she could find.

Konrad wasn't sure what to do exactly once he was upon her, and he felt faintly put off by the intimacy that lying on her would require and yet he felt compelled to follow through. 'You must copulate with me, then sign the pact!' Konrad stood over her a moment, expecting her to end the game, but instead she pretended to writhe away from him. Then he slowly lowered himself on top of her, in case she changed her mind, part of him hoped she would.

She turned her head sideways, lightly pushed at his shoulder. 'Oh no, I couldn't.'

To which Konrad answered, 'You are under my control now,' and felt her bony hips rise. He followed what she was doing, and rotated his hips against her, where exactly on her body he wasn't sure, her hip? Thigh? She made little noises, sighs and moans of refusal, but it was still part of the act. He didn't notice his breeches had slid down from the rubbing motion, or that her skirt had ridden up. But suddenly he knew for certain he was against her thigh; he could feel the heat of her skin.

Then, just purely by accident, somehow he felt something even softer than her thigh, even warmer, something he could feel unfold, even under the barrier of her undergarments.

'Ouch!' she cried out, and pushed him off. 'Oh, look what you did. Oh, oh, oh.' She touched herself and held her hand up in front of him. 'I am bleeding! Look what you did!'

Kneeling now, Konrad grabbed her hand and inspected it closely, but couldn't see any blood. 'There isn't any blood, Juditha – what are you talking about?' He half smiled, not sure if this was part of the scene. But he was already filling with terror that she was not pretending.

'Oh, yes there is.' She looked again, deeply, into her hand. 'I am bleeding inside, and you did it.'

Konrad couldn't take it, he felt pressed in, his airways constricted, he wrenched her hand up to his face, even closer this time. 'No blood.' And there wasn't, not a single drop.

She snatched her hand back and brushed straw off her

dress, then stood, waiting a minute, as if expecting some kind of explanation from him, or worse, an apology.

'I don't want to play this any more,' he said and turned away from her, looking for something to seem occupied with, settling on the bottom of his shoe.

She left meekly, believing he had somehow drawn blood from her.

Konrad stood up, the heat still gathered there in his groin. Alone, he could replay what had just happened: the warmth of Juditha's thigh; the fact that she wasn't bleeding. Why did she have to be that way? Why did she always have to go too far in her little performances? He didn't even like her, really, he only went along with it out of boyish curiosity and because he hadn't any sisters to satisfy it with. Didn't everyone peek at their sisters, at some point?

He was often frightened after she left, and would look around the stable a number of times half-expecting a real witch to come out of the shadows and say to him, 'Well, if you're so interested I can take you to the sabbat now,' and her hair would swirl round her head like a demonic Medusa. At other times the building heat he felt would beckon him, such as it did on this afternoon. He thought only of what they had done, how it felt, before the supposed blood.

His hand wandered over his breeches, and then slipped inside them. There was always a moment of perfect denial about what would come next, for Konrad had heard many times in church that 'If your right hand causes you to sin, cut it off and throw it away. It is better for you to lose one part of your body than for your whole body to go to hell.' So in order for him to pretend this wasn't sin, he had to say to himself he was just scratching his inner thigh, and as he did this, his arm would bump against his shame, again and again and this motion would eventually bring him to a dry shudder.

Johann, an apprentice to a draper, had told Konrad once, behind the church, that his penis squirted milk. They were near the same age, and Konrad wondered if something was wrong with him that he had yet to produce this substance.

So many things went through Konrad's mind during his 'scratching', fragmented thoughts of Juditha, a prettier, larger-breasted version of her, of the woodcuts with naked women touching one another and sometimes of these women turning on him and forcing their hands down his pants, visions of the side of Anna's head against the cow, the movement of her hands, the slight quakes that went up the back of her head as she pulled milk from the cow. He thought of Johann doing what he was doing now. These images were much like a deck of cards being shuffled at lightening speed only to have wild cards turned over and exposed at equal speed, then shuffled back into the deck; different images each time. Images he seemed to have no control over.

Such odd thoughts, thoughts that seemed to be conjured

up on their own, thoughts that were very unlike him and afterwards, when the residue of pleasure still lingered, he would feel utterly perplexed when he paused to consider them.

But mostly he didn't. He liked to dive into some task right afterwards, and forget all about it.

Too lost in his approaching climax, Konrad didn't hear the gentle scuff of footsteps, the quick tapping of a forefinger against something dense, a dull ting, ting, ting that subliminally played into the urgency he was feeling.

He saw the bowl first as it dropped from his mother's hand breaking into large pieces on the stable floor. He moved outside the scene. As his mother knocked her fists against his head and shoulders, he stood perfectly still, allowing it to happen. Not a single protest brushed past his lips.

He struggled to pull up his breeches, and tuck in his shirt, as if he were simply getting ready for the day. He was able somehow to withstand his mother's slaps and punches without uttering a single word, perhaps because she didn't either. If she had offered him a tirade of insults, of threats and chastisement, maybe he too would have said something back, an attempt at an explanation. I was only scratching myself, he would say, I was just itchy. But her silence made it all the more unbearable for him to speak, so he just closed his eyes and seemed to float above the assault his mother was inflicting on him.

It wasn't until she left that he plummeted back into himself, and embarrassment and shame rushed over him like a biting rash. He tasted blood; his bottom lip was bleeding. He stood in silence, a good while. He heard the plop of a horse's bowel movement, the stench of the stable rose up round him with new intensity. Then, suddenly, he doubled over and cried out, an open-mouthed guttural growl. The image of him doing what he had been doing would for ever be emblazoned in his mother's mind. He knew she could never again look upon him without seeing him committing this act. He would never simply be himself in her eyes, but would always, always, be tethered to this. The fact that the image of his mother against the cow came to him during his perversion, was as if he had willed himself to be caught by her, as if he had willed it that she materialized in the flesh right before him, as if she knew he had thought of her during such a repulsive and wicked act.

This was a cataclysmic event, worse than famine or disease, much worse than hail that tore apart every vineyard, because it was his catastrophe alone. There, in the stable, he was alone.

Something had been ruined, he knew this, ruined between him and his mother.

As this knowledge settled in and he finally absorbed it, he repeated it over in his mind and felt a growing sickness in his stomach of self-disgust and loathing. She knew for certain now that he would never measure up to Manfred's goodness. He hoped that she would one day find Manfred doing the very thing he had just done. He wished it.

As more time passed and Konrad remained slumped against the stable wall, he began to see the injustice of his mother's reaction. Why was it that she could so easily forgive Manfred's many deficiencies, and yet she found him just once engaging in something deficient and she could not forgive him? By this point Konrad had decided she never would, even after years of enduring and abetting her lies about Manfred. He should go straight into the tavern and tell his father everything. But he knew it was too late for that, no one would believe him, not after today. He should go over to the saw and lop off his right hand, and for the next few minutes he imagined the gory scene of himself walking into the tavern, blood spurting everywhere, shouting, 'I will never sin again', or something to that effect, and Manfred being pushed aside as all the patrons became enamoured of his mother's other, repentant son.

As anger built up inside him, he could actually feel himself lighten, as if the weight of his mother's expectations of him, began to dissolve one by one. There was freedom in this, he thought, to accept fully his mother's disgust towards him. He no longer had to go about pleasing her, vying for her love. He could just be what she thought of him now, and be liberated from ever caring again that she loved Manfred more. Thinking about it now, in this mood, he realized that perhaps his mother and Manfred were both knowingly conspiring to trick people into thinking his brother was holy, was seeing God in a spoon.

In fact, they had even tried to dupe him. He ruminated on this for a while, but couldn't quite master the idea of a life without wanting to please his mother. So he turned his thoughts towards Juditha, to her insidious ways of getting him to play her sacrilegious games. If it hadn't been for her, none of this would have happened. He transferred the rage he felt towards his mother to Juditha. It was her influence that had brought him to this. Now nothing would ever be the same again. Nothing at all.

# CHAPTER 18

Anna went round to the small narrow alley on the other side of the tavern, where patrons went to urinate. The pungent reek of urine was overpowering, but she was only faintly mindful not to step too far for fear of wading into the small streams. She felt bewildered, and wanted some time alone to compose herself before going back into the kitchen. How could she have one son discovered, only hours before, to be a godly healer, and the other discovered in the stable in the throes of sin.

A sudden tide of sorrow overwhelmed her, and she could not prevent tears streaming down her cheeks. She had to hold herself up by leaning one arm against the mossy brick of the tavern. It felt like loss, this sorrow, as if someone near her had just died.

For seeing Konrad that way brought a sudden feeling of estrangement. Her son was no longer an extension of herself, no longer her little helper with Manfred and in the tavern. He was an individual with his own secret desires, his own mysterious yearnings and such things predicted what sort of a man he would turn out to be. She knew nothing about this part of him and was quite surprised that it existed. Wasn't he too young to struggle with this? He still looked so much like a little boy to her; she couldn't reconcile this with her son feeling lust.

And the act itself, my God, the act was deplorable! It could ruin him both morally and physically. She would tell Wilhelm later, and he would have to talk to Konrad about the necessity of self-control and the repercussions of self-pleasure. It was a sin, an insult to God to do such a thing without the sole purpose being to reproduce, it could bring sterility, blindness, lesions on the face. It simply ruined one's moral compass. It led one astray to hedonism, so that the body reigned over a person more than God. This was not what she wanted for him, to be some seeping hunch-back in the streets with his hands down his pants. A perverter of God's gifts.

But she knew she wouldn't talk to Wilhelm about it. No, she never wanted to talk about it. How could Wilhelm teach his son self-control when he had none himself? She wanted to drive it from her mind. She planned to remind Konrad discreetly to go and make his confession and do penance so he could repent his sin. She also planned to hire a stable boy – they had the money now – and Konrad could work exclusively in the tavern where he couldn't get away with such things.

With this strategy in mind, regardless of how unformed it really was, she was able to stand upright again, smooth down the front of her skirt, and go back into the tavern. She noticed Juditha in the kitchen. Elsie was demanding something of her and Juditha was trying her best to keep looking anywhere except at her stepmother. She turned away from her, in full defiance of the scolding she was receiving for suddenly disappearing. Anna suspected Elsie was doing this more for the benefit of the others in the kitchen as she usually welcomed her stepdaughter's absence. Then Anna noticed bits of straw clinging to the back of Juditha's dress and hair.

As the afternoon faded Anna went to wake Manfred, to wash his hands and face, readying him for his night's stay in the wake-house. She found him already awake and sitting neatly on the bed, his legs folded underneath him. Upon entering the room, Anna was suddenly filled with hesitation, unsure how to approach her own son. She felt reluctant to touch him, as if to do so, would wreck the reverence she had felt for him earlier in the church and then downstairs all afternoon in the crowded kitchen. As if to touch him would turn him into a tactile, ordinary being. She wanted very much to retain her reverence for him. There was something so comforting in the inevitably of it all, she thought; there was nothing she could have done to prevent it. Manfred would always have been born as he was; they were always on this holy path and their previous existence was always leading up to this. Dare she say that she too was chosen, Wilhelm also, by God?

Yet as she advanced into the room, and under the weak light coming in from the window, he looked nothing like a miraculous child. He sat there, dumbly, picking at something behind his ear, not noticing her at all. So she spoke out loud, out of habit in the hope that Manfred would pick up on it. 'Let's get you washed.' But she sounded strained, false somehow. Or maybe it was just not a reverent thing to say. It would be better to wash him quietly, leave him to his thoughts, whatever they might be.

She urged him to stand up, turned him towards the chamber pot in case he hadn't gone already – and he did need to go. Who helped him with such things throughout the night? It was not the first time this had crossed her mind, but she liked to believe that while inside the church God led him through such ordinary tasks, and when he was home, God knew she would. It must be how he manages it, she assured herself.

Once he was finished, she stood him up on the stool beside the table and dampened the cloth in some water and gently rubbed his empty hand, and then his other hand, round the golden spoon he still grasped. He had slept with it. She could see herself in the spoon; she looked squat and bloated and this startled her. She would have expected to look different, or that she would radiate light.

As she brought the cloth to his face, he began to push her hand away, and tried to step off the stool. This was always a fight, to wash his face. Washing his hands was always easier, he would relax, his breathing slowed as he watched the water run over the backs of his hands and between his fingers.

She held the back of his head firmly. His legs kicked out into her legs, his knees went into her stomach so she had to wrap her whole arm round him to bring him tightly against her so he couldn't move. 'Stop it, Manfred, just stop! It will only take a second.' But it was no use, she was only able to clear the sleep round his eyes and wash part of his cheek. He started his fake sneezing, forcing air sharply through his nose so snot bubbled down over his upper lip. She struggled to wipe this too, before finally releasing him. He dropped down onto the floor, onto his back, using his feet to push himself across the floor, as he made the strange bleating noises he was prone to in these states of agitation.

I don't understand, she thought again and again, as she stood there, watching him.

The door opened, Anna lurched towards Manfred to pick him up, but it was only Konrad. She expected him to shut the door again upon seeing her, but instead he walked right in, stepping over Manfred's legs as if he were an inanimate obstruction. He hadn't come in for supper, and Anna would have to admit that she had been quite relieved at that. She felt perhaps that he was administering self-penance, allowing one's hunger to go unappeased as punishment for the appetite he had sated.

'I need a blanket,' he said flatly and walked towards the bed. 'Can I take this one?'

'What for? Take it where?' It was taking all her strength to get Manfred up off the floor. Was Konrad planning to cast himself out? Stay in the stable? But Anna did not hear any remorse in his voice, any shame, which she found off-putting to say the least. She had expected that the next time she saw him he would be so meek he would not even speak to her, never mind make a demand. She hadn't the patience for this right now, with a tavern full of people downstairs, with these few last hours with Manfred before sending him back to the church.

'We're to bring our own blankets, if we can,' he said, as if this was an explanation. Anna noticed how strange his voice sounded, it was so flat, so dull. He stood by the bed, facing the wall. What was he looking at? For a moment he seemed like Manfred, staring so vacantly at the wall.

Finally she had Manfred cradled awkwardly in her arms. She went and sat down on the bed, holding him like an oversized infant. Konrad was looking down, running his hand over the top of the bed.

'For what? No, the blankets are for the guests, you can't take it.'

'Fine, then. I better go soon. I am to take him back with

me.' He nodded towards Manfred and Anna swore she saw a flicker of delight go over his face.

'Go? Where are you going?'

'I've been seeing witches, Mother. A witch has been telling me to do things I don't want to do. Telling all of us.'

'Witches? Who? What do you mean "all of us". Who else?' Anna moved Manfred off her lap and onto the bed, where he continued to lie on his back. He was at least quiet.

'Juditha and Caspar. Juditha when she's with me in the stable, and Caspar when I sometimes help him in the cellar. The witches try to take our wine, but we defend it, you know.'

'Konrad, listen to me . . . Juditha goes into the stable with you?' Of course. For a moment she couldn't speak.

'That is why I've been feeling so possessed lately, and why . . .' He stopped; she knew he wanted to say it was why she had seen him abusing himself earlier. 'I am to stay tonight in the wake-house, Father Gottlieb said so, for protection. He said Caspar should come too, considering that witches have been in the cellar.'

'You've talked to Father Gottlieb already?'

Konrad looked directly at her, perhaps as a challenge, as if to say there was nothing she could do, she couldn't prevent him. But it seemed he hesitated into a kind of pleading, as if he wanted her to stop him, make it so he didn't have to go.

★

Anna walked with her children to the church. She had let Konrad have the blanket and he hugged it close to his chest. It was much later than she usually took Manfred and so she carried him to keep a quick pace. It was already dusk and dark enough that she needed a lantern. No one spoke. When they reached the church, Father Gottlieb was waiting at the doors like a fretful relative.

'Frau Wirth, you're late!'

As they climbed the steps he hovered over them.

'You're late,' he said again, expecting some kind of explanation. Anna only looked up and nodded, but couldn't bring herself to apologize or offer an excuse. Konrad and Caspar reached Father Gottlieb before her. He quickly shuffled them in, beyond the church door that was propped open by two bricks, into the glowing mouth of the church.

His arms were already out ready to take Manfred from her, but Anna hesitated.

'How long before they can return home?' She was slightly breathless from the climb.

Father Gottlieb shifted impatiently, and again started to reach for Manfred and then it seemed, he changed his mind.

'I cannot say for certain, only God knows, but there has been great progress here. You have nothing to worry about, Frau Wirth, this is the safest place for your children until the threat of witches has been eradicated—'

A shriek from inside the church momentarily cut him

off. It sounded like a cross between playful and pained. Anna looked past him, but he stepped closer and blocked her view.

'And this one,' he said, looking at Manfred, 'has made the best progress; he does so well at catechism.' He spoke unnaturally loudly, Anna believed, to overwhelm any more noise coming from the church. With a tight smile upon his face he leaned in towards her, and pried Manfred from her.

Once he had Manfred in his grasp, he turned away and started to push at the bricks at the door with his foot.

'You shouldn't be out so late, it really isn't safe,' he cautioned her before closing the door behind him.

# CHAPTER 19

Konrad remained just inside the vestibule, hesitant to go further into the church, but still taking care to be far enough away from the door so his mother couldn't see his reluctance to go further in. Konrad tried to hide his embarrassment from Caspar by looking down at his feet, as if straining intently to listen in to the conversation outside between his mother and the priest, though it was obvious that nothing could be heard clearly because of the noisy din coming from the nave. When Father Gottlieb entered and pulled the door firmly shut and locked it, Konrad was momentarily besieged by a sudden urge to pound it down and return to his mother. He pressed his back against the wall. He didn't trust himself; he needed to feel anchored.

'Come, come, blessed Manfred.' Father Gottlieb strode by appearing not to notice Konrad but then called out from the nave, 'And where did your brother get to? I just hope he doesn't miss the play!' How different Father Gottlieb's voice sounded, compared to the austere voice Konrad had listened to that afternoon inside the confessional booth. It sounded strangely whimsical, feminine even, and was obviously meant to be overheard by Konrad and entice him further inside the church; a tactic normally used on much younger children. Still Konrad hesitated. This would be the first time he had ever slept away from home and suddenly the prospect inspired a flush of anxiety. He didn't want to be away from his mother or the tavern. He felt too loose, too unfocused, not in his thoughts, but in his very being – as if the outlines of his body had blurred and become imprecise.

It was the third time he had been at the church that day. It amazed him it was still the same day, it seemed so long and divided into so many different sections. Just that morning, when he woke, he had fully expected to go to sleep again in the very same place he had all his life. Never did he think he would be here. This added to the surreal sense that none of it was happening. His heart beat more and more quickly as if insisting it was.

It was Caspar's sigh, the way it caught in the back of his throat to give the impression of impatience that made Konrad go further into the church. It was lit with what seemed a thousand candles and was very warm, both from the candles, but also from the many young bodies brimming with excitement. Konrad noticed the children on the floor in front of the altar going through a small trunk full of hats. Some held wooden fish; three large pairs of sandals were being tried on for size; a shepherd's cane was being passed round; and two vestments with wings attached were being quietly fought over by two girls.

Father Gottlieb stood by the children going through the hats. He was laughing and had an overall giddy manner about him as he plopped the hats on some of the heads round him. His long finger tapped his chin in mock pensiveness. 'No, no, use this scarf to play Mary.' He removed a flattened hat and draped an old, ratty scarf round some girl's head, who Konrad didn't immediately recognize. Father Gottlieb glanced up then and gave Konrad a boyish wave.

The girl who had the scarf, which she was now unwinding from her face, turned also, and Konrad was stunned to see it was Juditha. She was sitting with some other girls on the floor near the open trunk. He wasn't sure what he had expected to happen after he made his confession to Father Gottlieb that afternoon. And, really, he had never thought about what would happen to Juditha, being so concerned with his own absolution. But seeing her there seemed a bit of a betrayal by Father Gottlieb. Slowly, as he walked in, he wondered what Juditha had said about him when she made her own confession.

As he walked down the centre aisle, Juditha stared up at him, and leaned back on her arms, just watching him. She looked as if she had left her house in a hurry; she was still wearing a stained kitchen apron over her ill-fitting Sunday dress.

'Quick, quick. We're about to begin,' Father Gottlieb called out and everyone struggled into the front pews. Those losing out hung their heads as they found a seat further back. Konrad sat in the pew closest to him, and so managed to be in the third row.

'What is happening?' he whispered to the girl beside him, who was kicking out her legs, causing her skirt to make a slight whooshing noise.

'Shh . . . it's time for the play.' The girl put her finger to her lips without looking at him. Her fingernails were filthy. Konrad guessed she had been at the wake-house for a while. He had noticed that those children who had been there for some time, had an unkempt and faded look about them. The play was being put on at the very front between the pulpit and the altar, but the pulpit had been moved off to the side, so there was ample space. Konrad assumed they would be watching some rendition of the yearly passion play.

It seemed that to welcome Juditha, Father Gottlieb had allowed her to choose that night's play. Unsurprisingly, to Konrad at least, she chose to play Mary Magdalene, from Luke 8: 2–3.

It had all the melodrama that Juditha usually relished, Konrad thought. But why wasn't she too hurt or too bloody to be in a play?

She looked as if she had pinched her cheeks to give her-self some red, and had done something to her lips to make them glisten pink. It was all quite effective, and she looked the part of a harlot as she traipsed around with one hip jut-ting out. Father Gottlieb said Mary had become possessed when she was just a child, and Juditha gave a little shudder, and continued her sultry pace. To draw out the scene Father Gottlieb described how Mary's wickedness began to feel like a burlap sack filled with stones, and Juditha's body grew immediately sluggish and hunched over. He also said she was diseased and covered with sores because of her sin-fulness and Juditha scratched at her arms.

When Mary finally met Jesus – played that night by a boy who, out of nervousness, could barely keep a straight face – in the streets, Juditha put on a riveting performance: falling down at his knees, clinging to his thigh, and tears, actual tears fell from her eyes over her cheeks that seemed sud-denly high and delicate, tapering to her exaggerated mouth. Her movements were fluid and natural, she had none of the stiffness of her acting partner; instead she alone enticed her audience onto the streets with Mary Magdalene.

Konrad suddenly found he wanted to play Jesus next to her Mary, and was horrified that his earlier arousal had returned. He shifted uncomfortably. He had not told Father Gottlieb everything during confession, he had held back the parts that made him look bad, the parts he just couldn't bring himself to say out loud. He hadn't really been absolved of his sinfulness and so was plagued by it again. His blame towards Juditha turned inwards instead. It is me, he thought, something is wrong with me.

Jesus put his hand atop her head to cast out the seven demons; Mary thrashed round on the floor, moaning unabashedly like a woman giving birth as the evil exited from her. Then she went suddenly still, and the light caught her forehead and Konrad could see a thin layer of sweat making her skin shine, and her cedar-coloured hair splaying around her head in small waves, having been unbraided for the role as prostitute. She had confessed everything. This was why she had been allowed to choose the play and not him, this was why she could act so freely now, and he envied her for it.

When she woke she raised herself up slowly, first turning onto her side, then leaning against one arm with her legs angled behind her. She maintained an expression of solemnity and bafflement, and in spite of the fact that her audience knew the ending, they were still filled with suspense whether she would be truly changed or not. Juditha seemed to be aware of this and prolonged the moment until the tension reached its apex. She finally declared herself eternally devoted to Jesus, and wrapped her head tightly up in the scarf Father Gottlieb had recommended earlier. Everyone applauded, which seemed an astonishing sound inside the church, but Father Gottlieb allowed it, even encouraged it, and Juditha stood forward and gave a quick curtsey, which Konrad thought was a bit boastful. As she stepped away, she blew from the corner of her mouth to cool her forehead, causing the stray hair that had fallen loose from the scarf to billow up.

It was only once her performance ended and she was seated in one of the pews that Konrad felt relieved of the sensation of having held his breath for some time.

Looking back on his first night just days later, Konrad would be amazed at how little he remembered about it, other than Juditha's play. It seemed as if he had been washed up on the shore of a strange island occupied only by children, ruled over by an affable, pitying king. As the days passed and before they no longer seemed to pass at all but become one, long, single night, Konrad quickly adjusted to the routine. During the day the children slept until past noon, then woke and had some boiled oats – donated by the baker's guild – then spent the remainder of the afternoon split into smaller groups taking catechism, while another, larger group were minded by nuns from a nearby cloister, and put to work beading rosaries to be sold abroad, or boiling blankets as it seemed there was an endless tide of lice, or to aid making the supper stew, until it was their turn to attend catechism.

The church now remained closed to daily Mass, but for Sunday afternoons. Daily Masses were held in other churches, where, Father Gottlieb often reminded them, vigils were constantly being held for their recuperation.

In the early evening there was what seemed a lengthy period of free time, where everyone was able to go into the church kitchen and have some diluted wine and some stew to eat – with meat donated by the butcher's guild. This was a confusing affair, but the nuns were there to ensure everyone had an equal portion and took their leave shortly afterwards so the children were alone with Father Gottlieb.

Father Gottlieb conversed casually with everyone after supper, asking what they had thought of last Sunday's Mass, how they had slept that day, what games they liked to play; questions most had never been asked before. This aroused in most children a feeling of self-importance, of being their own separate entity away from their parents and siblings and what they felt were the endless tasks being asked of them.

There was a lot of chatter, and nearly everyone vied for Father Gottlieb's attention.

A play would be decided upon. These nightly plays formed the centre of the day/night of life in the wake-house. They were like a beacon in the darkness, the highlight of the night.

Father Gottlieb let the children decide the Bible story they wished to depict. To make this choice was the most power they had ever wielded before in their short lives. It caused a considerable amount of anguish to decide between the more popular stories – like Noah's Ark – which had been chosen six times already – and something original that had not been done before. Costumes were agonized over, and gestures practiced.

Father Gottlieb would read the chosen Bible passage out loud, keeping pace with the children's actions, slowing down when one stumbled or needed to recover from a bout of shyness. If something went wrong, for example when Friedrich dropped the shepherd's cane and it fell in a loud clatter to the ground, rather than discipline him, Father Gottlieb only stifled his laughter, giving permission for everyone there to have a good laugh at Friedrich's red-faced clumsiness.

Then when night had decidedly fallen, Manfred would open the prayer session with a song.

Konrad watched him, thinking he looked quite ridiculous standing there, his eyes looking upward, roaming around looking at nothing, but pretending to see heaven. Regardless how pretty his voice was, it also sounded desperate. Just to bear it, Konrad had to push his legs against the pew in front of him, so that the physical strain of it made the emotional intolerance easier to bear. At least until the person in front of him turned round and gave him a dirty look.

Manfred gave no sign of recognizing him, even when Konrad went right up to him. This further intensified his belief in how deceitful Manfred was.

The other children joined in the second or third hymn, depending on how long Gottlieb wanted to listen only to

Manfred. After this, there followed a lengthy liturgy of prayers that took up most of the night: repetitions of the Lord's prayer, the Ave Maria, the divine praises, the creed, the listing of the ten commandments, many psalms. Over and over. Other mantras were said that Father Gottlieb authored: 'The wicked are born to die, the good are born to live for ever', or, 'God causes sorrow for sins committed, and gives joy to those who cease to sin'.

Father Gottlieb walked along the aisles of the church making sure everyone said the prayers. 'Friedrich, I can't hear you!' he would call out and as a result everyone would speak a little louder. He seemed to randomly choose someone to make confession, just one or two a night, though he did favour those approaching maturation. He warned the rest that he would still be able to hear if anyone were to falter in their prayers, but there was little risk of this because by that time the children were steadily under the melodious spell of godly consonants and holy vowels, the repetition of which had the same mesmerizing effect as if they were speaking in tongues.

When those who had confessed returned, they seemed altered in some way, sombreness overwhelmed their pallid faces and they were eager to become lost in the nightly prayers. Thus the confession booths were an ominous presence and one was divided between fear and eagerness to be chosen, for at least there, one had Father Gottlieb entirely to oneself.

After the first hours of prayers, Konrad became acutely aware of his discomfort. He felt as if his kneecaps would splinter, that his throat, his dry, dry throat would also splinter and the prayers would come out of his neck sounding like the high-pitched sounds of a reed. He felt stiff everywhere: his elbows, wrists, the fingers of his clasped hands. Exhaustion wrapped itself round him like a warm embrace that tried to pull him back into the pew. Just when he felt himself give way and his body slacken from the kneeling position and lean sideways into the invitation of sleep, he became enveloped in the murmuring chorus around him, and his body went numb, his mind blank. His mouth moved independently, his eyes remained open on their own. He became part of a larger body, and became only aware of others in the church whose bodies were verging on sleep, the way one does when their foot prickles when asleep. If they were not able to stay awake they fell away from the large body like an amputated toe.

They were lost then, Father Gottlieb said, let them sleep now. And so they slept, and so they were taken. When they returned, they startled awake; they always startled awake. Father Gottlieb would rush over to them and they would recount their abduction.

The prayers would continue, but everyone would turn to face the child who was speaking. Yes, they floated out from their bodies, first they felt hands on their shoulders trying to get a grip and then pulling out their souls like a tablecloth from under a table setting. They soared, and here description was important, the sensation of being lifted, the wind, the stars, the tops of houses. What they rode upon was pored over: the backs of wolves, a giant feather, or even most bizarrely, one was carried to the sabbat on a tooth he had lost the year before, though it was as tiny as his fingertip.

It should be said that there was a great amount of competition between the children in having their dreams deemed impressive by Father Gottlieb and by those around them.

You knew the dream was a failure if Father Gottlieb listened and, when the dreamer was finished, only blessed him and did not press further for more information. This meant the dream was conventional: a dance in the forest round a fire, a banquet of delicious food, the devil wearing his green huntsman outfit, with his green hat with the green feather, so no clues to the identity of the witches could be extracted.

It quickly became clear, that only those who could offer variations on this grand narrative could hold the attention of Father Gottlieb and earn the awe of his peers. Of course, too many improbable contrivances could render the dream a simple nightmare, inauthentic.

The dream had to follow an arc. Ignorance in the beginning – 'I didn't even know I fell asleep' – to fear, then resilience and finally escape. Here too, there was an airing of injustices one had previously endured and could now finally voice. Someone took their slice of cake and ate it, just like their older brother had last St Niklaus' day – not that they were going to eat it anyhow – no one admitted to eating the food at the witches' banquets, though it always looked delicious, and this too was pored over in great detail. One child stated that a witch had scratched her arm, and hissed in her ear that she better not tell anyone, just as her older sister had last month.

The witches dismembered everything, from beautiful singing birds to infants; there was much blood. The Host was trampled on. Women crawled on top of one another, grinding their pelvises together, or women on men, or men on men, or the devil on all the men and women. Some pushed babies out of themselves then ate them right after. The devil took on many guises, from goat to dog to horse to pallid old man to a beautiful woman. Eating faeces made a constant appearance, especially when the devil made the witches kiss his anus. The anus too was a running theme, one child saying he saw the devil put candles in witches' bums. Konrad knew this was lifted directly from woodcuts he'd seen at the tavern, but he was still lost in the horror of it all, for it could only mean that this was a common action of witches. Candles were soon replaced with torches and then sticks to hang lanterns from.

And so, yes, children flew to the witches' dance on missing teeth and not brooms, the devil took on all sorts of

222

forms and the witches engaged in all sorts of depravity, all kinds of obscene acts. There had to be variations; the appearance of objects from one's home, the chair from the kitchen floating mid-air, being forced to carry out tasks they disliked when they lived at home, like emptying chamber pots or fetching water. This was what made their abductions authentic, what made them so unquestionably real, the personalization of their accounts.

The dreams soon evolved, until the children were no longer running blindly under a blanket of darkness. Faces were seen. And who did they see there at the witches' dance? The much dreaded seamstress with her curse-laden mutterings and her loathing of children, the tanner's daughter with the horrid cleft lip, the exhibitionist midwife who may have helped birth some of them.

Then there were those who did not wake up at all, but remained trapped in their dreams. They resisted all the pulls and pushes to wake, or would seem to wake but spoke in evil tongues, sitting upright in the pews. Father Gottlieb would sprinkle them with salt and holy water, and finally, Manfred was brought forward, and just like he did with Herr Zwenk's daughter, he would stand beside the victim and eventually touch his spoon to their face. Sometimes Father Gottlieb had to guide his hand, but this never ruined the spoon's effectiveness, for the possessed would quickly recover. Never did the spoon again completely banish witches from entering one's dreams and this Father

Gottlieb could not fully explain, only saying that God worked in mysterious ways, but he believed their own faith was being tested: would they always choose Him over who they saw at the witches' sabbat?

Still, to be touched by Manfred's spoon was considered an enviable experience that enhanced one's traits in the days after, like a new pair of shoes would add to one's height, or a pretty ribbon could add shine to one's hair, and this led to a small number of fakers, who were not clever enough dramatists to feign demonic possession. Father Gottlieb showed no outward sign that he recognized a disingenuous possession; he would go through the same ceremonial regimen, perhaps because to admit one child could be lying meant that any of the children could be lying and this would undermine the whole operation of the wakehouse.

But children are always much more transparent to one another.

It was not to say that Father Gottlieb allowed the children to run wild. If one spoke to another during prayers, he would punish them by smacking their open palms with a thick leather strap. 'Just like God, I show you immense love,' he would say afterwards as the child whimpered and held his hands in his lap, 'but also, like God, my love for you cannot always be gentle.'

The rest of the children would side with Father Gottlieb, not their bruised peer, because it seemed he did not want to do it, that the child had forced him into it so they felt bitter towards the offender.

When the sun began to rise, and after Manfred had sung his last hymn, Father Gottlieb would pick him up, and go into the rectory believing all the children were asleep or, at least, on the brink of sleep. Manfred slept in the rectory, segregated from the others and where, it was believed, he slept on a mountain of pillows and was served any cake he wanted. But he would not eat too much of anything, it was decided, he was too good to be greedy.

The nuns would return and begin to prepare the oats for when the children woke. But there was always a window of time, its length varied each early morning depending on when Father Gottlieb left and the nuns arrived, but there it was: time alone, inside the church. A burst of frenzied excitement that came from lack of sleep, from being still for so long would always start off as celebratory. They made it through another night of wakefulness, stillness, and those who had slept and been abducted were still alive and well.

A sense of freedom was wonderfully realized in the very early morning, as the children in their exhaustion lost all sense of time. Excited children rolled and slid over pews, or crawled on the floor, a game of tag would be started and then quickly modified into something rougher, tag that required pinching instead of just touching, and then eventually this too would turn into a complex game of warring

armies. Elaborate games of hide and seek were also played.
There were many places in the church to hide: behind the
statue of Mary, under the altar table, inside the confessional
booths.

Girls rushed over to one another, and spoke in low, mysterious whispers, glancing round anxiously to see if anyone
could overhear them, followed by uncontrollable fits of
laughter.

Manfred's apparent ignorance of Konrad's presence
reduced the status he had previously enjoyed behind the
church. So much so, that some of the children had forgotten he was Manfred's brother at all.

Nonetheless, it seemed that Konrad's reputation as
intrusive and annoying had not followed him into the
church and he eagerly joined in the games that went on,
and because of this he was happy. He was quick to lose
himself completely in the physicality of it all, after feeling so
mentally bound up – running, skipping. Father Gottlieb
never woke or came back in to chastise them, it was
assumed because he could not hear them. Sometimes
Konrad would think he saw Father Gottlieb, standing in the
hall that led to his rectory, just watching them, but the grey
creamy light during this time between night and day played
tricks with the eyes.

Eventually this burst of excitement became diluted with
exhaustion and a sullen mood took over. Quarrels broke out
and sobbing could be heard from the youngest children,

who missed something or someone from home, their mother, sister, their rag doll. Accusations of children plagiarizing dreams were flung about and the children who were believed to be faking demonic possession just for a touch of Manfred's spoon were teased, pushed, and they curled up on their section of pew and tried to fall asleep quickly, losing out on any remaining fun. Gradually the children would fall into the pews like a giant creature, slowly, but finally succumbing to the arrows pierced into its body.

And then it would be day.

# CHAPTER 20

'Look at me, I'm Maaaary Maaaaaagdelene,' Johann
squealed at the front of the church in a high-pitched, feminine voice. He had one hand on his hip and strutted back
and forth, running his other hand through his hair. 'I just
can't stop myself from being sooooo wicked.' He had the
scarf Juditha had worn and ran it over the back of his neck
with overstated flamboyance.

The props were not cleaned up until the nuns arrived,
and this allowed Johann to stage mockeries of earlier plays.
He mimicked the confusion of the youngest ones, the mud-
dling of lines, all the mishaps, like Friedrich's dropping the
shepherd's cane, 'Oh, clumsy me!' or the time when one
boy playing Joseph turned round and walked away from the
Star of Bethlehem. The children were divided over how
they felt about Johann's 'performances', some thought it
was just harmless fun, others found it crude and tried their

best to ignore it. No one, however, told Father Gottlieb about it, for fear they would no longer be allowed to put on plays.

It was Juditha's depiction of Mary Magdalene that garnered Johann his largest audience.

Konrad turned to watch Juditha's reaction. She tried to look busy by running the ends of her braids over and over her palm, as if she were painting some faraway scene.

'Oooooh, ooooh . . . Jesus please help me,' Johann moaned as he seductively rubbed his hands across his chest. Then his hips began to gyrate as if they moved independently from the rest of his body, forcing him to clamp his hands against them to try and prevent them from moving. He continued in this feigned battle for some time; it was met with a swirl of laughter.

Johann made Juditha's performance seem trite, hollow and sexually inviting. He stripped her emotional performance, making it nothing more than a series of exaggerated facial expressions and body spasms. Even Konrad felt it was unfair.

Konrad had made fast friends with Johann. He was not the only one who wished to befriend Johann, many did. He was the sort of boy other boys admired. He was tall, with a thin layer of hair already over his upper lip and though it was often infected with small whiteheads, it was still impressive. He was the quick-witted, domineering sort, whose sole purpose was to find ways to amuse himself, and this untroubled, easy quality he had about him, was highly regarded, considering the circumstance. Konrad often found himself trying to emulate it, at times imitating Johann's obnoxious conduct. He'd even lately found that his laugh had started to sound like Johann's, taking on a sharpness that wasn't there before.

He was drawn to Johann for another reason as well. He knew he had committed the same sin as Konrad at least once, from what he had told him behind the church. But Johann seemed unaffected by his past transgression and when Konrad was near him he, too, felt less bothered by his own. Johann would regale Konrad and the other boys with accounts of the witches' dance, which always included bare-breasted women with acorns or strawberries or, even once, sheep testicles for nipples. It was a shared embellishment; Konrad knew this, because if it were true Johann would have told Father Gottlieb. This also quietly appeased Konrad's own inability to dream about witches. He had yet to have a single dream about the sabbat. Even if he tried to dream of it, the best he could achieve was an awareness of himself sleeping on the pew waiting to dream of witches.

Johann began to writhe on the floor, emitting high-pitched squeaks, which was, as always, his grand finale. Konrad always felt uneasy about laughing too much at Johann's little plays as Father Gottlieb had yet to choose him to be in a play, so although he was safe thus far from being parodied, he knew that could quickly change. Each afternoon his chest was tight with worry and anxiety that Father Gottlieb would say his name; he dreaded the thought of standing up in front of so many people and later being fare for Johann. But Father Gottlieb never did, and though Konrad was relieved by this, it also furthered his belief that Father Gottlieb knew he was guilty of an unconfessed sin or, when he felt less fraught, he believed he was just as overlooked here as he was at home.

Juditha stood and ran towards the confessional booths and disappeared inside. Konrad allowed himself to laugh quite freely then.

Johann brushed himself off, stood up and went on to something else and Konrad followed.


Later Konrad and Johann ran around tossing one of the sandals between them, and then hurled it at Friedrich, grazing his left ear. Eventually they made their way up to the balcony, where they hid from Friedrich under a pew. Friedrich, of course, had been hoping to throw the sandal back at them.

Konrad was becoming tired, but not Johann. He never seemed to tire naturally, but willed himself on. Konrad was quietly impressed by this.

They turned on their sides so they faced one another. Johann had started on already about one of his 'abductions' in a low, conspiratorial whisper, and this time he made the witches young. Some even bore a close resemblance to the prettier girls in the wake-house. They had all beckoned him, wanting to seduce him, wanting his seed to implant in themselves and have demon babies.

This reminded Konrad again, how much he wanted to ask Johann about the milky emissions he had told him about before. There had never been a good time, there'd always been other people near by, and Johann was never still for very long. Now it seemed a perfect setting to ask, being alone on the balcony. 'Does it really shoot milk?'

'What?' Johann scrunched up his face.

'You said that once, I don't know when, must have been about a few months ago, maybe more.'

'Said what?'

'Oh, it's nothing, I might have it wrong . . .'

'Ah.' Johann's face lit up. 'I know what you mean now.'

Konrad waited for him to say something more about it, but instead, Johann eagerly grabbed at himself, and said, 'Look, I'll show you. Just wait.'

He turned over, and Konrad watched the tip of his elbow pump up and down. He thought of the water pump behind the tavern, then of his mother drawing up water. Johann suddenly turned round, his hand still adeptly stroking himself, his legs twitching. 'Watch,' he hissed, and out it came, a quick spurt that resembled raw egg whites spilled onto his pants. He started laughing, and in the shadow under the pew, he seemed quite sinister, maniacal. He looked at Konrad expectantly, Konrad wasn't sure what to say or do.

He couldn't muster up a single word, and besides he felt suddenly hot and sickly and wanted to go down and sleep. He didn't realize how long he'd been quiet until Johann laughed again, but this time he sounded desperate.

'Want to smell it?' Johan dipped a finger into his semen, and pointed it towards Konrad who backed away, not laughing or making faces as he should have done to this gross gesture. He wasn't reacting properly and he knew it, but he couldn't make himself act any other way. And he could smell it, a vile fragrance of rotted pears and cheese. He recoiled further from Johann and his shiny, oily finger, and moved away.

Johann called out behind him, 'You wanted to see it, it's not my fault your little pecker can't do it.'

All Konrad could do was run down the steps and slip into the pew where he slept. He lay down on his stomach, pushing his nose and mouth against the back of his hand and taking short little breaths out of the corner of his mouth. Once he felt he could catch his breath, he burrowed his face into his blanket, and tried to smell the tavern. But it no longer smelt of anything familiar, only of incense and the oil and wood scent of the pew. There was nothing left in it that still held the distinct scent of the tavern, none of the ash and wine, and leather. It had all been boiled away.

He felt a sudden sting across his backside. He twisted round to see Johann hovering over him with the shepherd's cane. Konrad couldn't believe it; it was such a betrayal that

Johann would turn the shepherd's cane on him. He terror-
ized the younger boys with it, jabbing it against their bums,
declaring, 'You're Hans', then singing, 'Hans, Hans, was
stung in the bum, thought it was such great fun, until he
went and turned around and saw the devil had took him
down!' while chasing them round with it, until they broke
down in sobs. Sometimes, he used it to lift a girl's skirt up.
Now he was poking Konrad with the end of it, quite violently. Konrad tried to squirm away to the far end of the
pew, but Johann grabbed one of his legs. Suddenly other
children were on him, pulling at him, and he fell off the pew
onto the floor. Johann chanted, 'Hans, Hans, was stung in
the bum, thought it was such great fun!' Some of the boys
were holding his arms, while someone else attempted to
pull down his pants, but was only partly successful. But as
Konrad continued to try and wriggle away his pants lowered from the friction against the floor.

Johann continued poking him on both his bum cheeks to
a swirl of laughter and uproarious chants, 'Hans, Hans, was
stung in the bum . . .'

Konrad rolled back and forth as much as he could,
trying to avoid the cane. His legs splayed open as Johann
brought down the cane again and this time it caught
Konrad's genitals, pinning them to the floor. Konrad
screamed out in agonizing pain, pain that burst all the way
up into his stomach, to his lungs and throat, a shriek that
reverberated off the arched ceiling and walls, off the statue

of Mary, off Jesus' exposed ribs. His sight dimmed. He vomited.

Suddenly afraid, his tormenters retreated, Johann dumped the shepherd's cane by the altar and settled down into a pew.

Nothing else was said.

Konrad stayed under the pew, lying on his side with his knees drawn up to his chest. He saw two feet approach and stop directly in front of him. He recognized Caspar's battered old shoes, but still he did not come out from under the pew and Caspar eventually gave up and left. He supposed he should have felt a tenderness towards Caspar just then for being so loyal, but then he couldn't be sure that Caspar wasn't one of the boys involved.

How desperately he wanted to go home where everything was in order. He ached to be in the stable with the horses; he missed its earthy scent. He missed hearing his father's drunken drone in the tavern rise through the floor as he fell asleep. He missed his mother, how it used to be, how their arrangement to keep Manfred's condition secret seemed to seal them off from the rest of the world. For so long he had wanted to stop helping his mother care for Manfred, now he realized his life had had purpose then.

He heard a distant whispering which he tried to ignore; he was sure someone was talking about him. He covered his ears but even this movement added to the pain. He felt breathless, and it took much effort not to vomit again. The whispering sounded closer. He couldn't move to look and see if someone else was under the pew with him without renewing the severe pain in his groin. Still this small voice approached, he felt it now against his cheeks, his lips, in his own mouth. Prayers were circulating through him, one after the other, he couldn't stop saying them, he had to say them. Someone nearby told him to shut up, but it was entirely beyond his control.

Suddenly he thought, I deserved this. This was God's punishment. Not that he thought God Channelled himself through the likes of Johann, but that God arranged it somehow so Konrad would not ever sin again by touching himself. The agonizing blow had been delivered by God, for God's love is not always gentle, is that not true? Father Gottlieb said so. God was looking out for him, preventing him from going down the path of the wicked. Johann was only a pawn in all this because God saw Johann's sinfulness and did not love him. What had just happened was a way for God to teach Konrad the path of rectitude.

For Konrad, God had always seemed an abstract parent one had to placate by going to church and following its teachings. Just like his mother, God seemed to prefer Manfred, but now Konrad could see this wasn't true. This was why he hadn't had any dreams; he was in God's fortress and he didn't mean the church, but rather, he was directly protected by Him.

Something shifted inside him, something opened and he

was overwhelmed by it, by an absolute acceptance of God. He could feel God as surely as he could feel his own flesh, his own heartbeat. He felt reborn. God was speaking directly to him, saying, 'I've given you a second chance and you best use it to serve me, wholly and completely. My love for you will never falter because it never has.'

All the prayers he had uttered over the past weeks suddenly rose above the words he had memorized, even their rhythm became a chorus in his mind that sang loudly and gloriously. He fell asleep with a peacefulness he had never before known. While he slept, he dreamt of a hilly meadow speckled with sheep whose fleeces gleamed under the sun, and there, in his heart, an intense love for God unfurled.

# CHAPTER 21

Manfred was not allowed to go back to the tavern. It made perfect sense that a witch would attempt another attack there. This spoke of the intense hostility of witches for only they would crave to snuff out such a heavenly creature. It was too bad their other son had been caught in the cross-fire, but he was safe now. These reassurances were given to Anna over and over after Konrad's departure. This too was Wilhelm's philosophy. He had enough money now to hire a proper stable-hand and he hired another servant to help Margarethe manage the cellar, since there weren't any cellar boys around to employ.

It should be said, that by then little seemed to affect Wilhelm at all, for while the entire world seemed concentrated on staying awake, Wilhelm moved along in his usual wine- or better brandy-infused slumber. His consumption of brandy, now that he could afford it and had so little to do himself, had tripled, no longer was it a cup or two to get him on his way in the morning. He sipped brandy all through the day in between his cups of wine, which made his temperament especially hot and agitated. He was prone to interrupting other people, had no qualms about disputing another's opinion, and no longer bothered to endear himself to the customers. Just the other day, someone commented that cork was surely to replace oil-soaked rags as stoppers in wine bottles as it was beginning to do in France and this, for some reason, Wilhelm thought too incredible to believe. Who would want to eat tree bark with their wine? He went on about it for hours until the man quietly left. No one argued with Wilhelm, not about cork or anything else for that matter, because he was the father of Manfred, the child-healer, who saw God in his spoon. And this made Wilhelm very full of himself.

He took to trite little announcements, such as 'First one today', while tipping his cup of brandy or wine forward and saluting whoever was in the room. It made him look foolish because it was obvious that the drink he held was not his first that day. He would marvel aloud from time to time, 'If only my father could see the tavern now!' And he'd raise his glass in his father's memory, he'd do this with patrons or alone with equal fervour.

Most nights, exhausted in Anna's case, drunk in Wilhelm's, they went straight to bed and spoke only to one another in their usual sparing language. There was still the occasional night, when Wilhelm had it in his mind to want to recapture the intimacy they had shared the night they sat on the bed and were filled with anxious wonder that a witch had stayed at their tavern. But now, his focus was solely on their growing wealth. Anna would attempt it, sitting across from him, trying to make sense of his incoherent speech but was usually unable to. Eventually Wilhelm would become frustrated by his own inability to articulate his meaning, and would give up, grumbling his way to sleep. Even if he was coherent, she could not maintain the eye contact necessary for such intimate discussion because his face startled her too much. It's puffiness was so pronounced that it seemed his jawline receded into a soft slope that led down into his neck. And his skin – oh, how his skin was constantly sheathed in oily sweat and the sour odour of wine came from every pore. These attempts, she knew, were often meant to be the pre-amble to more physical intimacy, which she supposed tested his own ability to overcome his impotency. Always the wine won, and Anna was always relieved it did.

Her love for him had faltered. It was no longer an accepted fact of her life that she loved her husband. She was beginning to feel something very unlike love striking her during the rare and brief lulls in the day. But she was too busy, too full of grief for her absent sons, to think too long on anything but that elusive future date when they would return to the tavern. Then, she was sure, Wilhelm's drinking would be less.

The tavern remained busy, having not suffered by Konrad's claim to have seen witches in their cellar, which was made public in the broadsheets soon after he was interned at the wake-house, for witches were sneaking into everyone's home. There had been arrests, and those arrested were of no surprise to anyone: the tanner's daughter with the cleft lip, the impoverished seamstress, the exhibitionist midwife. These were the witches who had plagued the children in their dreams, and this was perfectly acceptable to everyone who resided in the city. Obvious, really. And while the tanner's daughter and the impoverished seamstress were undergoing torture, they revealed two others who were witches: a syphilitic mother and daughter who, it was rumoured, sold themselves as a two-for-one deal.

So overall, the arrests were satisfying. Many people went and gave their statements, linking their own personal misfortunes to these wicked women: an ailing infant, an inexplicable fire that razed two houses, a missing necklace.

But the children did not stop dreaming. They were still being abducted and this was more terrifying because now the obvious witches had been removed from the equation, who among them still abducted the children from their beds? No one knew who to suspect. Hans had not been a typical witch. They reminded themselves that a witch could be anyone and so everyone was to be mistrusted.

The walls of the city pressed them together like salted

fish in a jar, eyes perpetually open, watching each other. The streets narrowed so it seemed one could never have enough room to pass another. Small talk was avoided, but if it were to be exchanged, you then walked away analysing the nuances of every uttered phrase.

At the tavern there was speculation about customers not present, and when they arrived, and others left, those who had just left were also scrutinized. Old arguments and disagreements over property issues with a neighbour were discussed, and the suspicion that perhaps something more diabolical was in effect with their adversaries was mooted. The patrons in the tavern divided themselves up, so that small groups of two or three men sat huddled together, wary of saying too much to the wrong person.

Children still in their households were kept indoors, so as to keep them out of view of witches who passed as ordinary folk during the day. It could be anyone, the butcher, the baker, the blacksmith, or more aptly their wives, it could even be an aunt or uncle or servant. So the streets became devoid of children and their excited laughter, their hurrying or idle strolls, their frequent emotional outbreaks.

The city fell into a silence so profound that at certain times of the day the only sound one heard was the flow of the river.

St Niklaus' day passed as any other day, but for the afternoon Mass. Anna missed putting dried fruits and sweets in her sons' shoes, she usually put a little in Caspar's as well.

Caspar and Konrad both understood it was Anna who put them there, but not Manfred. She missed watching him carefully and very slowly extract the items inside his shoe, laying them all out before him with such precision, then spending the rest of the day sporadically pulling off his shoes and looking inside, as if there were invisible tunnels in the toes or heels that channelled these gifts into them.

Songs were not sung on the streets and Mass was in the afternoon rather than the evening, where Anna foolishly waved each time Konrad glanced back or Manfred sang.

It was best to keep their children out of sight and Flusstal seemed a childless city.

This was how the rest of the winter passed.

When the first hint of spring wafted through the city, and temperatures rose, and the sap began to concentrate in the pruned canes of the grape vines, pilgrims made their way to Flusstal.

They came in on the River Necker, first from small villages and cities just north of Flusstal, from the Catholic towns of Rottweil and Oberndorf, and then even further, from as far north as those Protestant cities, Esslingen and Stuttgart. Catholic minorities living in mainly Protestant cities gleefully gloated, 'See, God prefers to be loved passionately, not with your muted, unadorned Protestant worship. Was it not a Catholic child whom God showed His mighty self to?' They would join the procession to Flusstal with a new lightness in their step, and a triumphant smile, certain that this revelation caused a tremor of doubt in the Protestant's conviction.

The news of Manfred and his spoon, had spread east to Ochsenhausen and Wald, and south all the way to Einsiedel and as far west as those villages on the River Rhine. The pilgrims came on horseback and by foot, until they reached the southern end of the River Necker and then boated up the river. What a sight it was with so many boats docked along the river banks, like an infinite trail of stepping stones, filling the streets with life again.

Better than a cross that sweats, a statue of Mary that cries, or a glowing painting of Jesus, Manfred was a living miracle. It was believed that just hearing him sing, would lift one high into the heavens, and that a single touch from his spoon would bring health to those left behind at home too ill to travel.

The pilgrims filled the Holy Cross church on Sundays and covered its steps the other days of the week. After Sunday Mass Manfred would be set up at the front of the church, in his small black robe. When he wasn't singing, separate exorbitant amounts were paid to be touched with his spoon. After, the pilgrims would claim to feel renewal rupture in their heads, then chest and they were sure they would find their loved ones restored to health when they returned home. Those who suffered, but were able-bodied enough to make it to Flusstal, fell backwards after Manfred rested his spoon against them, and when they rose they felt their crooked feet straighten, their hearing and sight improve and would leave weeping tears of joy. Those few who were not healed, prayed vigilantly to be free of their anger, and have forgiveness for their sins, so that Manfred's spoon might work.

Night after night the inn was completely full. Pilgrims paid the same amount to sleep in the stable as for a room. Wilhelm started selling wine that had been blessed by Manfred for six times the amount of a normal cup.

It was a strange combination: travellers coming and expecting an encounter with God, while the residents wrestled with the devil.

# CHAPTER 22

Too many dreams were being had that didn't produce a clear and vivid image of who attended the witches' dance.

Since the arrest of the seamstress, the tanner's daughter and the midwife, the children seemed to have fallen into a lull. They were unable to clearly identify their captors, though they could lucidly describe their despicable acts. This seemed the great strength of the witches – to be able to terrify the children with their faces always concealed under shadowing hoods.

Even those rare glimpses of a face resulted only in the sense of a face that was familiar, but which you couldn't put a name to. One face could be composed of an aunt's nose, a shopkeeper's ruddy skin, like someone they knew, but then not like them at all. Some children kept seeing the same faces, again and again, and yet had never seen them before outside their dreams. Perhaps, the sheer numbers of children now in the wake-house made this failing seem especially pronounced; each evening a handful more arrived. Father Gottlieb had the idea that the children should sleep less and go out of the church around midday and onto the streets and search for these nameless faces.

Konrad sat up, sleep still clung to his eyes. They had been woken earlier than usual by the bells, and all down the pews the air was punctuated by yawns.

Father Gottlieb followed his announcement about going outside with a sermon on the Children's Crusade four hundred years before. 'When children, yes, children much like you, rose up and sought out the Holy Land and planned to convert all Muslims to Christians along the way, they were being called on by God, they were being led by the Holy Spirit. And with such holy purpose, they set out and crossed the Alps by themselves, all by themselves! Just children, just like you. They were infused with God's word, as I believe each and every one of you are infused with God's word.

'You are the mighty crusaders now, you are knights and kings and queens in God's eyes, you are little Marys in Saint Mary's heart, and you will weed out these soulless aberrations and so end their evil-doings. Rise up!

'Whatever is hidden away will be brought out into the open, and whatever is covered up will be found and brought to light!' Father Gottlieb called out this line from the Gospel of Luke, as they filed out of the church.

A sort of vertigo came over Konrad upon first stepping out from the church. Going down the steps, seemed a descent into an alien world. The bright light of the midday sun was an assault on eyes so used to the subdued light inside the church and this only added to the unfamiliarity and sent some of the children back up the steps, Konrad included. They wanted to get back inside, but no one dared knock on its doors and confront Father's Gottlieb's disappointment.

However, this loitering on the steps, even furthered the strangeness, because this was where their parents stood and conversed each Sunday. The nuns waved them off. The church would now be open daily to the pilgrims paying to see Manfred and they wanted the steps cleared. They told them not to return until the supper hour.

So they left the steps and circled behind the church first, as if there they could reclaim those lost days when they had played so freely, and knew for certain what the rest of the day would bring. When they came round to the front again, they half expected to see their parents, standing there waiting. But of course they were not. Maybe it was then, that that first wave of abandonment rolled inside them.

Finally they set off, away from the church.

They all walked together for a while, meandering

through the streets like a river broken free of its dam. They walked neither quickly nor slowly, but awkwardly. Their legs felt stiff as if with the onset of rickets, but as the sun continued to warm their cheeks their young blood began to course more vibrantly in their bodies. When Konrad looked round at the others, he was shocked to see how pale everyone was. Their eyes appeared supported by the purple crests underneath them, as if resting on tiny rowboats.

Oh yes, how nice it was to feel the sun's warmth, even on the crown of his head. Konrad's hair was infested with lice, and he hadn't washed or combed it for longer than he could remember. He hoped the warmth of the sun would burn the lice right out of his hair, and then all he'd have to do was find a place to hang upside and shake them out. But that would be for God to decide, whether he should have lice or not. This was how much Konrad had given the affairs of his life over to God and he was quite pleased with himself when he punctuated the end of his thoughts this way.

So they walked on and, though it wasn't said, there was an expectation that life outside the church had been interrupted without them; that the world would only again resume when they were part of it.

But the season had changed and the streets were full of unfamiliar people.

They went unnoticed at first.

★

249

Konrad considered yet again what he deemed the two thorns in his side. The first was that he kept pleading with Father Gottlieb to allow him to be an altar boy. But Father Gottlieb never answered, really, just told him to observe the altar boys during Mass. And Konrad did observe; he desperately wanted to be one of the torchbearers, to hold one of six candles for the procession and during the Gospel reading and consecration. Even more desperately, he yearned to ring the bells after the consecration of the Host, his hand even moved while the bells rung out. So involved was he in his observations, he rarely looked behind him any more, and when he did, it was never to look for his father or mother, but to watch the exiting procession of altar boys.

Father Gottlieb focused even more of his attention on Manfred now that so many pilgrims were there to witness the miracle that was his voice and spoon. A miracle! How ridiculous, thought Konrad, and I am prevented from serving at the altar of God, while my brother runs around like a false prophet. Before, Konrad might have blamed this unfairness directly on God, but now, he waited for God to right the wrong and knew, beyond a shadow of a doubt, this would occur soon. Any day. Maybe even tomorrow.

The second thorn was that the stain on Johann's pants had dried to a crusted outline round an oily smudge. Whenever he was near, Konrad could not help but look there. It taunted him, this reminder of his own dryness, and worse, his past sin. This stain, the sight of it, the knowledge of its existence, conflicted with his new view of himself as one who worked only in servitude to Christ.

So when Johann and his growing posse of boys veered right towards the river, Konrad decided to trail behind Juditha and the other girls. He wasn't the only boy to do so, but the other boys were younger, under seven or maybe eight, but he lingered far enough behind that he didn't seem to be following. He was rather dismayed at the thought that he couldn't go off on his own, but he put that behind him quickly by telling himself that most likely he would have gone this way anyhow.

They were at the market now, moving through throngs of people. It was louder than he remembered it; the influx of the pilgrims had obviously improved business. The air was laden with wonderful scents of leather, smoked meats, new silky fabrics, damp wool and even the dank smell of the river, but Konrad missed the stinging scent of incense. When he came upon an overturned crate he stepped atop it and looked up at the large clock on the city hall building that loomed over the market. He wanted to know how many hours there were until he could return to the church. Oh, how long this day would be. Already he was filled with impatience to be inside the church again, to be praying. As he looked out on the crowds, he thought how animal they appeared, greedily bartering for material possessions, when they should have been praying for spiritual wealth. How

251

they subverted God's will by idolizing Manfred. And now they were off, shopping in the market in a state of false piety and peace. He felt disgusted by the very sight of it.

Then he saw Juditha, who was easily noticeable, as she was the one still body in a sea of motion. Konrad followed her sightline. Her stepmother and beloved father were walking together in the market. Elsie carried the infant and her father was resting his hand on top of the toddler's head, an affectionate gesture he always gave Juditha. Elsie pointed at something, and Juditha's father leaned in, likely to hear her better, as his hearing was not what it once was. Elsie turned and put her lips close to his ear.

Juditha thought she was the one who should be walking with her father, either as the toddler with his hand riding the top of her head, or as Elsie, mother and wife. She loved her father so greatly, that her love belied that ordinary title of daughter. She believed he could not get along without her. She'd been expecting him to come to the wake-house all this time, to forcibly knock on the church doors and request that she come home. He would curl up against her, as he sometimes did, and hold her firmly against himself. A firmness that she always took to be possessive. Yes, of course, he had had to marry Elsie, it was expected that no man remain a widow for long, and he had put it off much of having Juditha at home with him; having her to find solace in. She could cook and do the wash as well as her mother by then.

She thought that when Elsie arrived, they would go on as they always had. That Elsie would more or less hold the role a servant would in the household. But they had not. Instead Juditha was relegated to servant, pushed to take care of the new offspring, to clean and cook. And how Elsie loved to ignore her existence, as if doing so could obliterate her. No, she did not deserve to just go on happily.

In a fit of violent jealousy and rage, Juditha went towards her stepmother, nearly sprinting the short distance and screamed, 'You, you, you.' By the time she reached her, her voice had broken with guttural outrage that cut through the whole of the market causing it to go still. Then and there, carters halted abruptly, causing their wares to tumble out of their carts. Those on the verge of selling shoes or shirts or salted meats or woollen blankets to a nearly convinced customer, went silent. Even stallholders reaching out for payment would later report their hands became paralysed.

Into this silence, Juditha simply proclaimed, 'You witch.' She did not yell, but said it in an even tone, and still it was heard by everyone there. Of course, the wicked stepmother!

Three or four men grabbed Elsie and held her until the city bailiffs arrived. Women held onto Elsie's two wailing daughters, and Juditha's father protested, but quickly found it was useless.

Her father turned towards Juditha, dropped on his knees, and pleaded with her, presumably to take back what she had said.

'I will come home, Father,' Juditha answered. 'I will take care of you, as I did before, and I will care for the babies.'

She reached out to touch him, but he recoiled and Juditha's hand dropped limply at her side. She seemed to consider something for a moment, maybe to accuse her father too, but then she stepped back and when she turned round, her eyes glistened with tears, but a satisfied smile played about her lips.

So in less than half an hour after the children left the wake-house, the first witch had been accused and taken. The quick arrest of Elsie spread quickly among the children and from there, their purpose was no longer an abstraction.

There would be no happy reunions between child and parent on the streets. Men and women averted their eyes as they passed their sons and daughters. Women pulled their shawls – though it was far too warm to wear shawls – across their mouths. Men kept their hats tilted forward to obscure as much of their face as possible. What would their children see in them now they were autonomous from them, what mistakes had they made that might have infiltrated their sons' and daughters' subconscious, and would they dream it?

So the children felt they were indeed rejected and abandoned – it had been six months after all since some of them had seen their parents; except on Sundays, and these had only been quick glances from the front pews. Why had their mothers not run over and embraced them, or their father swung them around? Why all the weak smiles? The estrangement from their families only pushed them further into the ready embrace of the wake-house.

# CHAPTER 23

Once the children were set loose on the streets, hazy dreams soon became clear. Faces came to light. It was the old widow who scolded the children for knocking into her as they ran by. It was the carpenter who walked by them and did not comment on their beautiful singing. It was the butcher who refused them smoked meats and the baker who didn't give them any cake, and the wine seller who declined their demand for something to drink. Whether the children did this knowingly or not, was at first a point of contention. It was argued that only those who wished to hinder the children's campaign would not offer their charity. It would soon become clear, however, as more people were affected by the children's bite, that perhaps malice was indeed at work.

By June the children lined the streets like marauding soldiers and everyone feared them. Simple peasant children,

cunning street urchins and the sons and daughters of arti-
sans and craftsmen easily mixed together. They were of one
single order, a guild made up of moralists, diminutive
guardians of God's grace. They operated with the single
goal of ensuring salvation for sinners. The children, ever the
most powerless in any society, were aware of this rare gift
that had been bestowed upon them. They alone had a share
in God's plan, they alone were elected to implement it. Rid
the city of evil and thus the city would thrive.

Oh, how they would eat their cake today and save none
for tomorrow. They would only ever do just enough to get
by, survive the single day they knew for sure they existed in
and worry about tomorrow when it arrived. It never made
sense to live any other way. With God on their side, they
were sure to have cake again tomorrow. And it was true,
they ate better than ever before.

Children could be seen sitting on overturned crates with
grease dribbling down their fingers from the roast meat
they held, eating refined bread with butter that melted
down their chins in a yellow river, cakes swallowed down
with the unhinged jaws of snakes. Beer and undiluted wine
were gulped in abundance and kept the children giddy
during the day and added to the impossibility of staying
awake through the night. Food and drink was given to them
in appeasement, for surely the children would dream well of
the benevolent baker, butcher and fruit vendor, or better,
not at all.

With God's grace, Flusstal turned into a city made of cake and marzipan and meat and butter.

A mother could step into another room but for a moment, and return to see her children had left. There, on the table would be the supper they had been preparing, a half-peeled apple, a half-sliced carrot, a half-grated turnip would be deserted. A bucket of water gathered to wash the floors would be overturned, flooding the hall, trickling down the stairs.

Even those children still in a household, and there were few, had long ago dissented, refusing to carry out their duties. A small daring smirk would play round their plump lips after their mother cuffed them in the mouth. Their fathers demanded nothing of them but right-mindedness, no requests were made to carry in firewood, to fetch this or that. How could one risk demanding servitude when at one's front step was mass temptation – children in the streets spending their days in vicious leisure?

If the day was sunny and warm, the children wished to be commended, as though they had cooked it up themselves, waiting to be told they were right. When adults passed by, they made sure to sing the famed hymn, or at least fragments of it, that Manfred had sang on the church steps that day. In those moments they still seemed like the children of before, their faces begging for a kind word, for encouraging admiration. What other proof need there be for a job well done, other than a clear sky, that the rain had receded back into God's wrathful palm, off to trespass on others, those other cities still riddled with sin and frail faith. If it rained heavily, with exceptionally high winds and the children were forced to creep under awnings and huddle under trees, it became clear how much work was left for them to do.

Hoops and ropes were also donated by coppersmiths and rope-makers and crowds of children raced their hoops down the streets, skipping in alleyways, pausing in their play only to glare at whoever passed by.

Those who had no gifts to give, tossed coins at them, as if it were an indulgence – hoping to buy salvation from their nightly reveries. Though coins, Father Gottlieb made it clear, were donations to the church and were to be brought back. He looked on those who brought back the most with such affection and commended them in a short announcement that glorified their triumph as if it were directly attributable to personal character. For example, 'Christoph – always the seeker of truth', or, 'Little Barbara, with great kindness in her heart'.

This inspired others to bring back more coins the next night. In place of the nightly plays, which had been given up on some time ago due to the overall disorganization that accompanied their ever increasing number, the children vied to be the recipient of Father Gottlieb's praises.

If it had once been lamented that the streets were void of childish laugher, it was now lamented that this was all that could be heard. The holy crosses that had been scribed in chalk on every doorway in an attempt to prevent witches from getting inside to their children, had changed in meaning and purpose; now it was hoped they would keep the children out. As dreams were being born in the children's mind, doubt was being born in the minds of the adult populace.

The outdoors was to be avoided for anyone over fourteen. When you did brave the streets you had to be sure to take enough coins to keep yourselves out of the children's dreams. And if someone still had the confidence to send their own children to carry out the necessary tasks at the market more often than not the children never returned.

So the children were much like a multi-headed behemoth and like the behemoth, they could only be destroyed by their creator – God. And so to speak out against this beast, these children, was to speak against God and in support of witches. The adults let it go on, only because of their belief that it would soon end. Each day they convinced themselves it would be finished by the following day, but that day too would pass unresolved.

# CHAPTER 24

It started in the morning and went on until the afternoon when the last headless body was flung atop an unlit pyre. They beheaded the witches this time; there were so many it would be too hard on the arms of the executioner to strangle each one.

Anna looked on in horror at the thirty-six women and twelve men who stood shackled, lined up behind the long platform that had been lengthened for the occasion. They were all naked and shorn, their bodies covered in various shades of bruising, yellowish fluids glazed over crushed hands and flattened lower legs. Their nakedness no longer distanced her from them, as it had with Hans, his father and Georg. She knew so many of them, and their exposure made them seem so intensely vulnerable.

The tanner's daughter had been shouldered out to the front by the others, she would not find camaraderie even in the face of death. She held her tied arms in front of her to cover her breasts, her cleft lip seemed to blend in now with the rest of her red and battered face and did not seem so menacing a feature.

The people were not jeering or telling lewd jokes this time. In fact the crowd was relatively sparse, even on this day when the children were not there; they would get to sleep through this.

Wilhelm stood solemnly beside Anna, and she believed she could feel him shrinking, as if he was pushing all the air out of his body so it too could disappear into the surrounding quiet. He hadn't expected this shift in mood, she realized, he believed it would still be a celebratory affair, and had hoped that his tavern would be full as soon as it was over. So now he stood awkwardly, and she imagined the frequent stiffness in his back made him uncomfortable, and that he wanted to go back to the tavern. He wanted to say he had to go now and ready the tables with pitchers of wine, and make sure there was some bread and stew ready. This of course was code for wanting to sit in the cellar, where it was dark, and he could be alone and drink copious amounts without his wife or anyone else knowing. He wanted to feel the tingling burn of liquor sweep through him and settle in his groin. His hands shook, as he brushed away droplets of sweat gathered round his nose and upper lip. Anna took some satisfaction in her husband's discomfort.

The list of crimes for each witch was read out loud, but this too failed to inspire any vocalized ire in the crowd. The only time the crowd broke from its silence was when Manfred was brought out on the platform. A collective sigh of relief was emitted, as if the angelic boy would somehow be able to set this right. Anna expected a hymn or a soothing song. Manfred's spoon was fastened to his slender wrist and it swung back and forth like a pendulum, catching the sun as it swayed to the right. It was hypnotic and upheld their faith that God was there, right there, just in the hollow of the spoon a few feet away.

Father Gottlieb blessed himself, as did all those in attendance, and took the hanging spoon and placed it firmly in Manfred's hand. If Manfred touched a prisoner's forehead, then it was true that he or she was a witch. If he did not touch them with his spoon, it meant they were not witches and would be set free.

The convicted were brought forth, one by one and pushed to their knees in front of Manfred. Moments passed, as Manfred seemed to consider the person placed before him by looking upwards and consulting with God. And then, his spoon descended as he pressed it into the foreheads and let it drag gently over the cheeks of the convicted, just as lethal as the sword would be a few moments later.

'You've been condemned by God for the malice you've committed and so your body must perish. Let Him have mercy on your souls.'

Anna knew that she was not wicked, was not in league with witches and so this motion of Manfred's spoon was completely meaningless. When the spoon had been deemed to heal, Anna had been filled with certainty that all those times when Manfred had touched her face it had been out of love, to heal her of the worry she harboured over him. It was as if he was saying, 'Mother, do not worry, I am fine, just not in a way you understand yet.' And this made her love him even more. It meant nothing now. And for a moment Anna mourned, for she realized it had never been a gesture of affection from him towards her. It meant nothing.

How does one even begin to manage the weight of this realization?

It meant nothing. But this could not edge its way out past her lips. She was a spectator, a mere witness to tragedy, powerless and yet her silence was the very cause of it. She could not speak up. What would she say? That Manfred had touched her with the spoon, often in fact. Would that not just put her up there on the platform too? How could she know for certain? Maybe she was wrong. Maybe all those people, there on the platform, were indeed witches, even Herr Hueber who always offered her a compliment on the most tepid of stews. Even Frauline Walz, the fruit vendor's daughter, always a pleasant young woman, but maybe underneath that pleasant veneer there lurked the evil-doer? Was it not said that her fruit was cursed and caused illness? And Frau Merk, could she not have always been so generous with what she charged for washing laundry, only to have access to others' personal belongings and to cast her spells?

Maybe they were agents of corruption, maybe they had danced with the devil and they wept now only because they had been caught.

And of course there was the seamstress, the tanner's daughter and the midwife – they must have been guilty. Everyone thought so. How could so many be wrong?

Anna tried desperately to cling to the belief that her son had been summoned by God, that this was not some accident, some coincidence, and her son was truly a guardian of the godly, of the good.

After being touched with Manfred's spoon, the witch was dragged over to the executioner and forced to kneel again. The sword swung high and came down. The sound was surprisingly subtle, dull – reminiscent of slicing an orange in half. Blood sprayed against the blue sky, like a scattering flock of small red birds.

Person after person went from Manfred's spoon to the sword. The bodies were flung atop the pyre below the platform, as if in pursuit of their heads. With each swing of the axe, Anna's whole body flinched, her own neck seemed to jostle loose from her spine. Anna watched each execution without allowing herself the luxury of looking away, of closing her eyes, of saving herself from the memory of this massacre.

Elsie was one of the last. Anna had somehow been able to avoid looking for her. When she was dragged out from the thinned group, shorn and beaten, she was hardly recognizable. Her body had been ravaged. Her breasts were covered with pincer marks, she had still been nursing before her arrest and Anna could see droplets of milk still oozed from her torn nipples, as if her breasts were weeping. Her arms hung askew at her sides, and seemed disproportionately long, as if her nakedness revealed an asymmetry to her body Elsie had always kept hidden, an inverted shrug. But the rope burns circling her wrists and elbows revealed that she had been subjected to the strappado. Both her shoulders were dislocated. It seemed only the loosened sagging round her stomach and her upper thighs remained unharmed, and so appeared sickly white, the softened underbelly of a dead fish.

They had no right to do this to her, they would soon see that. Anna suddenly had a vision of herself tending to Elsie, restoring her to health, wrapping up her injuries, feeding her hearty stews. She would take care of her daughters and take them to the water pump. Eventually Elsie would reveal the horrors she had endured and she would be changed, but alive and able to appreciate Anna's devotion to her recovery and their friendship would deepen. Maybe Elsie and her husband could take one of the rooms at the inn, Anna wouldn't charge them of course and it would be so much more convenient to bring her food, and water to wash her wounds. Even then Anna could deny what was about to happen, that the dire situation before her would have an entirely different outcome.

When Manfred pressed the spoon against Elsie's cheeks, then chin and finally forehead, Anna knew for certain that his spoon was powerless, meaningless. Elsie was not a witch.

For a moment Elsie turned and, while searching for her husband, her eyes fell upon Anna. She mouthed something that Anna could not make out. What had she said? Anna frantically pushed through the people in front of her and went towards the platform. She needed to know what Elsie had said. But Elsie kept her eyes only on her husband thereafter, and even as her head fell forwards into the pyre she retained a final look of desperate rage.

This collision between self-deception and a sudden awakening from it resulted in a feeling of madness or perhaps the departure from madness. Either way, Anna could no longer keep her thoughts straight.

The pyre was lit, and all those bodies would culminate in the blackest of smoke forming a suffocating canopy above the city.

Manfred began to sing. But no one there could find solace in his voice. Instead, he sounded different, smug, as if he were a miniature Nero playing the lute as the city burned round him.

No one stayed behind to listen, or to watch the pyre burn

the stack of bodies. Only Anna. Even Wilhelm, at the first opportunity, fled to his tavern.

And it was only Anna who heard Manfred at the close of his hymn, begin to sing letters, one after the other ... 'Beeeee ... Kaaaaay ... Mmmm ... Aaaaa ... Teeeee,' until Father Gottlieb took his hand and led him away.

# PART III

# CHAPTER 25

The tavern was dying a quick death. Anna could hear it
during the long stretch of time after the burnings when no
one at all came in to order a cup of wine. No one came the
next day either. Even the pilgrims were making a mass
exodus from the city, promising to return the following year
when the city was not so troubled.

The quiet was shrill. As if each faint tick and croak in the
walls was the tavern dispelling its last breath. If the tavern
was the heart of the city, then its pulse was weak and the
city was dying as well.

Sitting alone, in the drinking room at one of the tables,
she thought again about what Elsie had tried to say.
Suddenly she felt sure it was not a curse. After the burnings, Anna had been sure she had said 'Help us,' which
Anna took to mean to help with her children upon her passing. Anna had gone over to her house in the early evening

just to let Elsie's husband know she was available to help mind the children, but he had slammed the door on her. The fetid stench of an infant needing to be changed had wafted out, but was quickly overpowered by the sulphur stench in the air. Now, whatever it was that Elsie mouthed, Anna decided it had not been a plea for help.

Wilhelm called out for her, but she ignored him. Then he called for Margarethe. Last night, when the realization set in that no one would come to the tavern, Wilhelm had drunk himself into such a stupor that he had fallen down the cellar steps and broken his leg. Anna had found him at the bottom of the stairs, his leg curled up hideously behind him. A bone stuck out from his thigh, and his foot dangled from his ankle like a white limp fish off a hook. The doctor, who came out to set it, said that he would remain bedridden for at least three or four weeks, until it was set enough to use a crutch.

As soon as the doctor had left, Anna had paid an advance on Margarethe's and the other servant's wages and had sent them both away. She kept only the stable-hand, giving him a loaf of bread and three bottles of wine and forbidding him to enter the tavern for two days.

So now when Wilhelm called for Margarethe to bring him some brandy, she would never come. Anna had given him a small measure already that morning, just to even out the fever he was running, but that would be all he would get until the evening. It was a blessing in disguise, she said to him as he swore at her; she shut the door behind her.

Suddenly, she felt she could not stay still any longer. She couldn't listen to his next round of cries for brandy. She went into the kitchen and picked up her shopping basket and left.

Immediately on stepping out of the tavern she was again struck by the sickening stench of the burnt bodies. When would it go away? She was sure she could see fine ash floating in the air and falling onto her. She tried to brush it away, running her hands up and down her arms to be free of it, but it was no use. Whose ashes were on her? Was it Elsie's? The midwife's?

She turned Elsie's final mouthing of words over in her mind. What had she said?

Anna was glad she had taken her basket with her. She wanted to look purposeful, but a purpose to this walk had yet to form in her mind. She wasn't going shopping, no, now was the time to hoard the money they had made, they would need it. If she passed someone, she looked down into her basket to avoid being recognized as Manfred's mother. Oh, why hadn't she thought to fill it with something? It would have added a layer of authenticity to her act of looking preoccupied. She did this as she passed the singing rose girls.

Anna walked down Lace-maker's Way, and thought of how she used to linger there and run her hand over the lace

273

and would consider all the places that just a bit of lace could adorn, just a bit of lace could brighten, make a head seem to rest upon a cloud, a hand more gentle with lace at the wrist. In the past weeks she had actually ordered two new lace coifs, both had been offered to her by the lace-maker's wife for a nominal fee in exchange for Manfred to say a prayer for her sickly infant. Anna took this offer, knowing she couldn't get to Manfred to ask him to pray for this woman's child. She childishly reasoned with herself that she would eventually have Manfred do it and anyway, Wilhelm was selling wine that was not really blessed by Manfred, wasn't he?

Now, as a soft wind caught the white lace it seemed to shiver and looked ugly like a series of unfurled cocoons

Anna passed the cutlers and heard the jingle of a bell as someone entered the shop, the knives swayed on the strings that suspend them in the shop window like loose teeth. Normally she could smell the fish market long before she reached it, the putrid stink which emanated from the barrels of unblinking eyes staring up at the sun that would slowly rot the flesh, if not soon plunged into the waiting jars of distilled vinegar, but even here, the acrid odour prevailed.

She looked at the jars of pickled fish lining a long board, a school of watchful eyes that seemed set upon escape from their briny acidic ponds, from their softened flavoured bones, from preservation. Down an alleyway she saw some older boys with their hands up a woman's skirt saying they were searching for the witch's mark.

When she turned onto Purse-maker's Corner, it was suddenly like an overturned anthill, children seemed to just keep coming out from nowhere, as if from holes in the earth. An elderly woman was trying to make her way across the street, but the children were swarming around her, chanting, 'Gyp with mischief, fart with a bell, I shall go to heaven and thou shall go to hell.'

Each held their collecting cup up in the air like a spear, laughing uproariously at their churlish rhyme and filled with the power it brought. Anna had heard that they frequented Purse-maker's Corner most often, for those who could buy purses had gulden. But they knew enough not to stay too long in one place as ambush was necessary.

The woman dropped in a coin and tried to hurry on. She called out, 'Oh, how wicked to be caught on Purse-maker's Corner today.' She said nothing of the children, as if this were only chance, like catching the spatter of a chamber pot being tossed out of the window, as if these children were sprung from chaos and not the bones of her neighbours.

They swarmed round the woman, whom Anna now recognized as the widow Frau Amsel, a widow twice, her last husband was a mason and had died just a summer past. The children swallowed her down like a rising river. Someone threw a rock at her and it hit her leg, then another

275

which hit her buttocks and at this the children laughed hysterically, giving Frau Amsel just enough time to get away with an emptied purse.

Then they noticed Anna.

She dropped some coins in their cups and pushed them off, their backs damp with sweat that had run through their shirts. One leaned a moment into her touch, Anna pulled her hand away, his stumpy body too fleshy and hideous. In spite of herself she couldn't help but still fear that by touching them, some demon spirit would crawl up her arm and fester within her. She hastened past the rest of them, and as she did, she realized that Purse-maker's Corner had been her destination all along. She wanted to see if it had ended, if the children were back at home now that all the witches were dead, but they were still there. And still they would dream, until the city was void of grown-ups.

Suddenly, she knew what Elsie had said. It came to her in all its dreadful meaning, and it was the truth, the bitter, awful truth: 'This is your fault.' Anna staggered. She could hear it now, as if Elsie was there in front of her right then. 'This is your fault.' Something was pressing into her throat, she started to feel herself choking, it was the ash, she could taste it. She could feel the ash residue all over her, on her skin, in her eyes, her hair. She was running now, unsure in which direction she was heading in the twisted alleyways, but it didn't matter. She wanted to be away from the miserable smell of this smoke, from the ash.

The ground began to slope under her, and she slipped, lost her footing completely and skidded down the riverbank on her back.

She caught whiffs of the grassy earth, short glorious respites from the bitter smell in the air. The smells changed from one to the other as she skidded. The frustration, the utter feeling of loss and lack of control over her circumstance was exacerbated by the rapid polarities of the smell of grass and prickling stench. When she was finally able to sit up, she was hit with such dizziness that the sight of the river seemed a confounding mirage, as if the water was both rapidly rising and pouring over the shoreline, and yet dwindling so that the banks were the mere folds to a wrinkled dried crevice.

She sat there a moment, trying to regain some composure, fending off her light-headedness.

She watched a man with stooped shoulders on the tow path, trailing behind four horses, his whip limp and lagging behind him.

Embarrassed by the fall, she stood up and looked round to see who else might have seen her. She wiped her running nose against her arm and saw a strange figure a few yards to the left of her, jutting out of the riverbank. She couldn't quite make it out and yet it seemed familiar. Was it one of those awful dogs that sometimes lurked round the tavern looking for scraps of food?

As if she were offering herself to the figure, she went

towards it. But as she neared, she saw his familiar brown hair and the bend of his long neck. It was Konrad. He was kneeling down, deep in prayer. She would have turned round, if he hadn't been alone. When she spotted him on the streets she had avoided him. Like everyone else she was afraid of what he would accuse her. But now, she wanted nothing more than to take him into her arms, and hold him as if he were still an infant, and kiss him all about his face.

'Are you well?' she asked him this with such caution, that it came out as a broken plea. She regretted immediately that she did not say a simple greeting.

He startled awake from his prayer. 'Mother?' A wide smile broke out over his face. He brought his hand up to his brow to shield his eyes from the sun. 'I was just praying for you.'

He was pleased to see her, and this filled Anna with such relief that she sank down beside him. She took both his hands in hers. He gave hers a firm squeeze back, and she knew he didn't mind that she held onto him. He seemed so much like his old self, she thought, he was just looking at her, smiling. She sensed he was relieved too, that she had come up to him. Why hadn't she done this earlier?

'Will you come home soon? I want you to.' It was too soon to ask this, she should try and familiarize herself to him again, but she couldn't help it. Having her son again in her very hands, she just couldn't prevent herself from asking it.

'I want to, very much,' he answered, and Anna took him into an embrace and held him there. He sighed deeply, and his whole body seemed to go slack. They sat like that for a short while, saying nothing as the sun began its slow descent. She considered reminiscing with him, telling him little anecdotes of when he was a baby. They used to do this, though Anna couldn't remember the last time, but Konrad always appreciated these, the thought that there was a time in his life when he could not control his bowels, and unknowingly did terrible things like pull bowls off the table, giggling as they shattered – none of which he had any memory of. 'I did that?' he would ask, with incredulous curiosity, like a drunkard trying to piece the previous night together.

Instead she asked, 'What did you pray about?' She wanted to know suddenly what he had meant when he said he prayed for her.

He turned over in her lap, and looked up at her, his face a cold blue from the dusky light. For a moment Anna had a disquieting feeling of having her overgrown son in her lap. They must look so peculiar.

'I prayed for you,' he said again, as if it should make sense to her.

'To come for you?'

'In a way, I suppose.' Then he smiled again, which was

starting to be irksome to Anna, this knowingness about him. 'I prayed you'd see the truth about things.'

Anna took this to mean about what had happened in the stable, that she would realize he had lied about being taken by witches. Oh, how this explanation of his sinfulness had had its appeal for the both of them, how easily she had let him go. It was so much tidier than to think he had sexual yearnings. 'Konrad, listen, it will be dark in the next couple of hours, just go, please, and get Manfred and come home. There is some meat pie at home, and I can prepare a bath for you both.'

But he was out of her lap, and standing, looming over her. 'Do you really think it is up to you when I come home? Do you really think you wield more power than He does?' Rage flashed across his face, but quickly dwindled away into detachment.

'I only mean . . .'

Whatever intimacy they had just shared was over. He was not her son any more, now he belonged to whatever possessed him. There was a cool, vacant solemnity on his face.

'It is not up to you, it never will be. Nothing is. Don't you see that? Everything is entirely up to Him.'

He kissed the rosary he held and turned and walked away without looking back at her. She watched him until he faded into a speck and tottered up the river bank.

She stood, brushed the front of her skirt off, and started to walk towards home. In the distance she heard the reedy cries of children. There was a row of women laundering clothes and blankets in the river. They must do their laundry now when night was near and the children were busy scurrying back to the wake-house. They turned and looked at her, one by one. Anna could feel their scorn, though she did not allow herself to glance back and confirm it. She confronted it again just a few steps away, as the path by the river filled with more people out to conduct business that they avoided doing during the day. Each person looked at her with contempt and leaned in to their companion and whispered. She went up the bank and onto the streets. The shops that had been closed earlier had opened up and the lamps were being lit in their windows. It was worse here, there were more people and they deliberately bumped into her as she walked briskly past. The air was thick with their unrelenting susurrations, of which she would only make out fragments, but the meaning was the same. She thought at first their blame was directly solely at her, but soon she came to understand that it wasn't at her, but at Manfred. He was the behemoth that needed to be cut down.

She could feel beads of sweat gather on her upper lip, a dampness under her arms, a single drop of sweat rolled slowly down her back. Something brushed up against her ear, she tried to wave it away expecting it to be an insect but felt nothing, and yet whatever it was persisted until it crept into her ear. A dull hum erupted, a single, steady tone and as it penetrated deeper, she could hear it was not a wordless drone but a faint accusation played over and over. She understood then, what it was saying. She'd got it wrong. Elsie didn't blame Anna. What she had really said was, 'It's all his fault.' Anna could see her lips move, hear her, just as clearly as if she were standing right next to her. She couldn't even be sure if Elsie only mouthed the words or said them outright. This was what they were all saying, what they all believed.

It came to her then, what to do, what she herself must do, in a sudden and grave revelation.

She stopped walking and turned round towards the twin spires of the church, rising from the landscape like stony vines. It was the stained-glass windows she wanted to look at, the way they twinkled in the setting sun. She knew that if Manfred was in the church, he, too, would be staring up at the stained-glass windows, though she believed he would not be thinking of her. She again felt an affirmation that the plan she had devised was the only possible way to carry out what needed to be done.

It would soon be her son who would be deemed a fraud, sole cause of this upheaval. He would be burned or quartered, a fraud to be hung out. The dowser would blame the rod, Father Gottlieb would give him up, claim he had been misled by him. It would happen here in the streets. She was certain of what she must do.

It was on this day that Anna decided that she must kill

her own son, because he did not know what he had done and only she could provide him with a merciful death. She would kill him as gently as possible.

She would do it to be kind, out of love, to end the affliction.

# CHAPTER 26

Each time Father Gottlieb said, 'Please rise,' Anna feared the knife she had bound snugly to the inside of her leg would fall loose and clang loudly on the floor. Even so, she thought, if it fell out and made little noise, there was a good chance it would go unnoticed because she had a small pocket of space round her. No one wanted to sit near her. She was, at long last, the pariah she had taken such pains to avoid becoming. But it did not matter any more, she knew that as soon as she took her son's life, she would also be taking her own.

The knife pinched her inner thigh, and she had to shift her legs continuously to find comfort from its edge.

She thought of the pains she had taken to select it, running the tip of her finger against the blade at the cutlers. 'What do you need it for, Frau?' the shopkeeper asked, glancing behind Anna through the window to see if her presence was preventing other customers from entering. But Anna only said the knife she was looking for had to be perfect in its width and sharpness, and light enough for her to manage swift cuts. She ignored the shopkeeper's growing impatience and took her time. There needed to be a sense of ceremony around selecting the knife. She could have taken a knife from the kitchen, but it seemed important that it not be a knife she had ever used to slice an apple or cut a piece of bread for Manfred to eat. She settled on a narrow, serrated blade. 'Good for cutting leather,' said the shop-keeper and at this Anna nearly sank down to the floor. The thought that this knife would cut into her son's soft supple skin with so much ease, skin that would never grow the dark downy hair of manhood, or become creased and weathered or show nicks and scars accompanied with their own short history, was awful.

She had passed the last two days in a cold and unfeeling state so she wouldn't lose her nerve. She tended to Wilhelm, who was suffering from nausea and had conver-sations with patrons whom he believed surrounded his bed. She went over the tavern's books, and tried her best to bal-ance the next month's bills, and then wrote out a series of numbers for a new monthly budget. If Wilhelm was careful he could survive until, she hoped, the scandal had long passed.

When Wilhelm finally fell into another brief fit of sleep, Anna allowed herself a burst of anger and sadness. She tore down all the broadsheets and woodcuts and burned them in the fire. She allowed only one to remain intact: the woodcut with Herr Laumayer's and Herr Zwenk's rescued children gathered round Manfred. His mouth was a perfect oval that emitted lines that curled at the end to indicate his singing. She was there too, in the background, looking over her son with what now looked like assumed ignorance. This she re-posted on the tavern wall and spent a long time sitting down facing it as if by sheer will, she could step into it, exist there in the flat, one-dimensional world of the woodcut, where she still had the chance to change the outcome of things or better, just remain frozen there.

She stared at this woodcut until the fire finally dimmed to ashes, ignoring Wilhelm's shouts for brandy, and his continued discussions with phantom patrons, before falling to sleep, until bars of light began to slip through the shutters and slide down over the woodcut.

In the morning she brought Wilhelm a watered-down cup of brandy, some boiled oats and cheese, but he would not eat. She left it there anyway, just in case he became hungry later.

Mass started at noon now, and she made her dressing ceremonial. She took her Sunday dress into one of the empty rooms in the inn and put it on slowly, carefully, with the same kind of indulgence a bride would dress herself on her wedding day. She brushed out her hair, and rebraided it tightly, then pulled it under her coif. She was desperate to keep a sense of ceremony; it embodied her righteous love for her son and yet at the same time, it let her feel outside everything she did. She was not a woman who usually dressed slowly and ritualistically; she was not a woman who could endure such a sacrifice. This was not her at all.

Time was passing with extraordinary speed, Father Gottlieb's sermon was coming to a close and she realized she had heard none of it, just a sonorous echo. Each minute that passed brought her closer to her son's death.

She watched the back of Manfred's head, the way he was tilted towards the stained-glass windows. She saw his small fingers every so often grab the back of the pew, to help him twist just slightly to watch one window then the next. The light that passed through one of them made a colourful imprint of yellow and blue on his cheek, and then, perhaps by the passing of a thin cloud in front the sun, it looked more like a bruise before fading completely. Anna wanted to think it was the impression of the scourging of Christ.

He would go gently. She had to convince herself of this. He would be taken aback by all the blood, purely for its brightness. Whenever he had seen his own blood, from little scrapes and cuts, rather than cry indulgently he would dab his finger into it, and rub it between his thumb and fore-finger and study its fineness and the way it changed as it dried.

He might not even know he is dying, she thought.

Manfred was brought up; he was without his spoon. Anna tensed and sat forwards on the pew. Father Gottlieb touched Manfred's back and began to hum the hymn he wanted him to sing. But this gesture of his hand seemed too much like he was handling Manfred as a puppeteer would, and his voice sounded thin and desperate. There was a delay among those who bothered to kneel and Anna sensed they did so reluctantly, out of habit rather than belief in Manfred's holiness and those who remained seated, looked down into folded hands with restrained hostility.

Father Gottlieb paused, as if looking out over his congregation to see how much his amulet had weakened, and then as if to revitalize Manfred's effectiveness by example, he knelt down and his eyes filled with tears which he dabbed away by pressing his long fingers to his eyes. This did not get the reaction he wanted, and when the song ended, he stood back up rather awkwardly and rushed through the rest of the service.

All Anna could think of was that this would be the last time she would hear Manfred sing.

The children went out of the church first. Anna tried to catch Konrad's attention, but he lagged behind and only looked back at something indiscernible to her. He seemed reluctant to leave.

There was a short pause, and the rest of the congregation

began their slow exit, not wanting to meet the children on the church steps.

Anna knelt down and appeared to pray. She rested her head against the back of the pew in front of her, and listened for the last sounds of movement. She peeked through her folded hands and saw that the church was nearly empty, but for the altar boys tidying up.

They were distracted by their own whispered conversation. Anna stood and made her way towards the confessionals, glancing back once more, to ensure the altar boys hadn't noticed her. They hadn't.

Anna slipped behind the curtain of the middle confessional booth, and crouched down.

# CHAPTER 27

For a long while there was nothing, no sound in the church at all. The air staled quickly in the booth and she smelt her own breath, which was cloying and carried on it the bitterness of an empty stomach. She had not eaten or drunk anything since last night's supper for fear she would have to urinate.

There in the darkness of the booth, as the hours wore on, she felt as if she might not exist at all or as if she was a foetus, only faintly aware that it was alive. It was easier, therefore, to retreat from herself, not to think. She would have lost her nerve otherwise. Her hearing became heightened and any sound, perceived or real, caused her muscles to tense and feel stuck to her bones. Her knees ached from being bent and pulled up to her chest. She was sure the knife had cut her and she could feel the heat of blood, but she was too afraid to move and, more deeply, she felt undeserving of comfort and regretted adjusting herself earlier in the pew to relieve the pressing pain of the knife's edge.

Finally she heard the clearing of a throat, and something heavy was set down. Then Father Gottlieb's voice filled the church again. Anna startled, but remained still. She thought another service was beginning, or that the children had returned. She was puzzled as she hadn't heard anyone re-enter the church. She couldn't grasp how much time had passed. Was Manfred here now? Carefully and as soundlessly as possible she stood up and peeked through the edge of the curtain, though she knew she wouldn't see the front of the church from this angle, only the last rows of pews to her right and to her left the font of holy water.

The pews she could see were empty.

The priest's voice boomed through the church, 'I worry faith in God's plan for us is faltering. The devil is fighting us, don't you see? And you there and over there and here just in front of me, are willing to lay down your weapons. Why? Because you believe there have been too many casualties. Is this a reason to bow down to the devil and give him what he wishes? Are we so weak in our faith in God? As it says in Ephesians, "We are not fighting against human beings, but against the wicked spiritual forces in the heavenly world . . . put on God's armour . . ."'

His voice faded. Anna heard a strange scratching noise, which she quickly understood to be the sound of a quill on paper. He was writing his sermon and rehearsing it.

She couldn't tell if he had Manfred with him or not, and she waited for some reference to his presence. She pulled the knife loose from her leg and gripped it firmly but couldn't help feel as if she were play-acting. She clung to this, for then it seemed as if it weren't really happening, that it was too ridiculous to be true.

Father Gottlieb began again, this time with a wise solemnity. 'These are sad and dangerous times, and because the wicked never rest, the good are so very tired.' He yawned and let out a little laugh at the end of it. 'Let us not forget that we must bear God's will submissively, obediently . . .' Again she heard the scratching of a quill.

The idea that he prepared his sermon was not quite as troubling as the idea that he rehearsed its delivery. She supposed it shouldn't be. Of course he wanted to be well-prepared, but Anna had always thought his emotion was spontaneous, that his voice ebbed and flowed naturally in accordance with God's influence.

Finally, as if frustrated, he stopped, and she heard him mutter something, but couldn't quite make it out. He yawned again. Then there was a slow shuffle, and the faint, distant clicking of a door.

A short period of quiet passed, until some nuns came into the church. One was complaining of an ache in her shoulder, and another offered to ladle the stew into the bowls in her place.

The church then settled into another long silence broken

only by the faint clanging of pots and plates and the occasional thud of something being dropped on the floor. Firewood, perhaps?

The children returned, just a few at first, they giggled and moved round the church freely as if it were an open meadow. Then more and more trickled in, and the air became heavy with the smell of outdoors coupled with sweat and the faint scent of oily scalps.

She heard them talk about what they'd had to eat that day, their petty grievances with one another, the best way to play a certain game. The nuns ushered them in and out of the kitchen and she heard them talking about a mutton stew.

When Father Gottlieb finally returned, she knew he had Manfred from the discordant greetings they each received from the children. 'Bless you, children, bless you all,' someone else said and she wondered if it was one of the nuns. 'Come, come! Tell me, what did you find out, you who are the ears and eyes of God? What did you uncover? You, there, let me see what you have.'

Anna recognized the voice to be Father Gottlieb's. How strange he sounded, unlike she had ever heard him before. It was lilting and childish, and brimming with the unfettered energy of the children themselves. He charms them, she thought. She'd expected him to be overbearing, a vile authority figure who beat them into submission, but this was not so. They loved him and he returned their love. He offered the small boy he called forth nurturing compliments, and yet talked as if he were one of them.

A presentation proceeded of what individual children had accomplished that day. Four more boys were called up, one said he saw a woman who resembled a witch in his dreams, and he gave a physical description that was not familiar to Anna, ending with the amount of money he had collected. This went on in the same vein for the other three boys, the last one going so far as to say he believed he prevented a man in the grips of sorrow from turning to witchcraft. Father Gottlieb replied with a giddy, 'Bless you, child.' Two girls were also questioned but they sounded young and Anna heard only soft shy murmurings. Father Gottlieb did not linger so long on them.

Then it seemed these presentations were over. Anna couldn't tell if Father Gottlieb had again left the church because the children broke loose and the air was filled with shouts and games. They galloped up and down the stairs to the balcony like wild horses, a game of hide and seek was being initiated, but there was a loud argument over who would have the role of seeker. The absurdity of it – that the children were at play when they had caused the deaths of so many sickened Anna. She listened for Konrad's voice, and when she couldn't find it she tried to take solace in the thought that perhaps he wasn't totally lost to this madness.

The curtain billowed and Anna turned her knife towards it, ready to break free from whoever entered and

attempted to corner her, but then realized these undulations were only caused by children running past. She
rested the knife parallel to her leg. She leaned back, and
leant her head on her knees. When she looked up again,
the curtain still swayed and this had a slight dizzying effect
on her. She perceived a slight blotch in the black curtain,
like a small, faded half moon against a starless night sky
that seemed to wobble.

It took her several seconds to notice and then compre-
hend that there was a small face peeking in on her. It was a
young girl, only about five years, her face partially concealed, the other half was wide-eyed and smiling. Anna,
unsure what to do, pressed her finger to her lips and the
little girl let out a laugh, and let the curtain go.

Anna fully expected to be caught and became less careful by how much she moved the curtain herself to see if she
could find Manfred in the mass of bustling children. No
one noticed her, no one came to take her away.

'It is very dark. Come now for prayers, quick, quick,'
Father Gottlieb called out, and clapped his hands. This was
echoed by other children and Anna heard the kneelers
being drawn out from under the pews and hitting the floor
in quick, hammering succession. There were a few stray
coughs, and then Manfred's voice filled the church:

> 'Glory be to God on high.
> And in earth peace towards men of good will.

*We praise thee.*
*We bless thee.*
*We worship thee.*
*We glorify thee.'*

Not being able to see him, Anna could better perceive the rich quavers in this voice, and the delicate variations in pitch; these gentle pulses ran through her and, for the length of his song, she felt pregnant again with life. Her head rolled from side to side against the wall, as if cowering away from the intense love inside her. She couldn't bear to hear him. Her resolve was so weakened she felt almost confused as to her whereabouts. What dark crevice had she fallen into?

When the song ended she was relieved and the knots in her stomach loosened.

Finally the prayers commenced. At least they really did pray.

'Receive my prayers as incense, my uplifted hands as an evening sacrifice . . .'

The church was filled by a hissing noise, supplemented by discordant panting. It was a frightening sound because the children's eagerness could be heard in it. As they went on, the prayers began to resemble the sound of rushing water or the rustling of leaves in a tree on a windy night, and Anna felt subdued by it. Doubt began to creep in, and her thoughts turned to how she could carefully extricate herself from the situation she was in.

The thoughts were broken by the sound of approaching footsteps. The little girl had probably started to wonder while she prayed who the strange woman was hiding in the confessional booths. But the footsteps went into the booth to the right of Anna. There was a short rustling sound and then she heard the partition slide open.

'How are you, my son?'

'Well, Father, thank you.' The boy's voice was unsteady, with croaking overtones. Anna assumed he was close to Konrad's age, even older.

'Have you helped others become closer to God in recent days?'

'I have.

'Have you taken the Lord's name in vain or used profanity?'

'I've never said the Lord's name in vain, Father, but I did say damn three days ago when Joseph grabbed a stick that I was carrying too roughly and scratched my finger.'

'Is your sorrow genuine and authentic?'

'It is, Father.'

'Your nature is weakened by sin. Do you wish to grow up to be strong and healthy?'

'I do, Father.'

'Have you been chaste in thought and word?'

A long silence, which Father Gottlieb broke. 'Tell me about your last dream.'

'In my last dream, the devil took the form of a goat.

Three witches were atop it, and . . .' The boy spoke eagerly now, relieved to be on a topic that had less to do directly with him or so he thought.

'Were the witches naked?'

'They were, Father.'

'And did this cause you . . . any arousal?'

'It did not.'

'Do you always tell the truth?'

A pause. 'I do.'

'When you saw the goat, did you also see its penis?'

'I did.'

'Describe it.'

'It was long and red, and seemed as if it would be hot to the touch.'

'Did this cause you to think of your own penis?' Silence again. 'Do you wish to be on the side of the righteous? I cannot help you, my son, if you do not wish to be helped.'

'I am not sure. If I did, I was asleep.' The boy sounded nervous, hesitant.

'Have you ever secreted in your sleep?'

Again a pause and a barely audible, 'Yes.'

'Have you ever woken this way after being present at the witches' dance?'

'I don't know . . . No, I don't think so.'

'I want you to think very carefully now.'

'I suppose I can't say for certain either way.'

'Do you think it was the sight of the goat's penis that caused it?'

'No.'

'Tell me then, what caused your secretions?'

Again the boy delayed his answer. 'I do not recall.'

'Do you not seek forgiveness from God? Do you want to be pursued by wickedness?'

'I think a witch might have caused it.'

'If you tell me and make your confession, you can bring God's attention to it, and he can take it away from you. Now, was the witch male or female?'

It was not a confession, but an interrogation and the boy stammered through it, until he admitted to once feeling aroused when he saw his sister peeing, and this Father Gottlieb seemed to want to explore further. He wanted all the particulars: the age of the sister, when it occurred, time of day and so on. He commented that it was odd for the boy to be aroused at the idea of seeing something come out of his sister, rather than the thought of something going in. From there he became more excited, and the next series of enquiries took more or less the form of statements, so the boy only had to answer in the affirmative or negative. Eventually the priest pressed him to answer if he had ever hosted thoughts of penetrating an anus, be it with an animal, another boy or even his sister?

Anna was filled with a combination of bewilderment and revulsion. Initially, she couldn't be sure if she was reacting to the boy's admission or to Father Gottlieb's doggedness at attempting to extract such information. But, as it went on, she felt heat emanate through her, on her neck and back. Her throat felt constricted round the inarticulate cause of her terror; the booth was suffocating her.

The confession was interrupted by frantic growls, and a young girl calling out, 'She has a demon in her!' with the same enthusiasm as if she held a newborn kitten. The prayers increased in volume, at first Anna thought it was to drown out the girl's cries, but then they took on an even greater rhythmic quality. She heard them move and thought they must be circled, chanting, round the girl.

'Oh my, oh my!' Father Gottlieb said as if he were some nursing maid whose charge had skinned a knee. He began a series of Latin evocations. It was as if he was attempting to be all things to them, mother and father, friend and now, Anna suspected, something else entirely.

She now felt an intense urge to leave the booth; she felt suddenly empowered by her outrage and disgust. She opened the curtain. The children were a sea of bowed heads, clustered more tightly on the far side of the church, close to the possessed girl.

Father Gottlieb was standing over a vacant part of the pew, then she realized the possessed girl was lying on it. He shook his aspergillum over her, with quick twists of his wrist, but then drew it back and felt the outside of it. Father Gottlieb turned and went towards the centre aisle. He had

300

Manfred's hand in his own, and led him along by holding the aspergillum so that the perforated silver ball faced Manfred. It would seem like a giant spoon to him. When he reached the font he dipped the aspergillum into it.

Anna stepped out, quite carefully, not rushing as she had assumed she would. 'Give him to me,' she gasped, her throat was very dry and she was unsure she even said it out loud, because Father Gottlieb didn't look up and she went unnoticed for a few seconds. 'Give me my son,' she said again. This time he looked up, cocking his head to one side as if he hadn't heard her, or was trying to place her. He set down the aspergillum on the edge of the font, and stood in front of Manfred. Anna hated herself for it, but she felt embarrassed by this sudden exposure of emotion.

'Give him to me!' This time Anna managed to convey some sense of urgency.

The priest nodded at her, as if he had expected her all this time. 'Go now, and I will forget this, Frau Wirth,' he said very softly, his voice imbued with forgiveness and understanding.

'I only want my son. That is all, just . . . just give him to me.'

'But he doesn't want you. He wants to be here, serving God.'

The children in the back pews had noticed what was happening, and were slowly turning round. They tapped those in front of them and the prayers slowly ended and the contrasting silence startled Anna. She regained her composure and did away with the pleading in her voice. His denial of what was rightly hers, incited the necessary indignation in Anna to demand Manfred again, with the necessary aggression.

'Don't you realize, if you take him, you are just another witch? Don't you see that? Abducting your own son will only strengthen how deeply we are under siege by such malevolent forces.' He turned and called out, 'See, who this is children? Try and think if you've seen her before.'

The children had moved towards them. Anna caught sight of Konrad, but could not read his face. He still had his hands clasped and his lips continued to move.

'You're a pederast, you're perverse. I heard you, everything, trying to get them to talk about . . . such despicable things, urging him on for your own sick pleasure.'

'A pederast?' At this Father Gottlieb flushed red with anger and his mouth dropped open in outrage. His reaction was too exaggerated, too perfect, as if he'd been practising it. 'I am exactly the opposite of that, Frau Wirth. I care for souls, that is what I do. I am trying to prevent perversion. Do you not see that? I examine the children, their consciences, and when I come upon a potential for sin I try and extract it. I am preventing sin before it occurs.' He smiled smugly.

She couldn't move or speak. He was so willing to reveal himself because he wasn't threatened by her.

'You are such a silly woman, I always thought so from the beginning, and what is the knife for? To cut him up and eat him? Or will you boil him first. Here take him. I'll have him again tomorrow anyway.' He pushed Manfred ahead of him.

Anna lunged forwards and grabbed him, wrapping her free arm tightly round his chest. He squirmed and nearly bucked her off. Anna was so desperate not to let Father Gottlieb have him back she called for Konrad to take him.

Konrad looked up, his lips stopped moving, but he looked at Father Gottlieb not at her.

'Go on, Konrad, dawn is upon us anyway, take him home. I will collect you both tomorrow.'

Konrad gripped Manfred's hand and took him towards the doors, but didn't leave.

'Get out now, you witch. Get out of here.' The priest turned slightly to the side, and was about to address the children again, but something stopped him. There was a disconnect that happened then, between Anna's body and herself. Her body moved completely independently of her mind. When she stepped back, Father Gottlieb was bleeding from his neck. The blood sprayed out onto some of the children's faces and he briefly tried to pull at the knife lodged in his neck before falling to the floor. He was still trying to talk, but only emitted a series of gurgles.

Anna turned to run from the church, but the youngest children were upon her, implementing justice at its simplest level. 'Bad, bad!' they screamed at her. 'You are bad, bad!' They grabbed her feet and she fell under the weight of them, pushing and crawling on her. Once on the floor, they pulled her hair and kicked at her, and one of them, or maybe they took turns, punched her in the stomach and breasts. The older ones were on her now too. She saw their angry faces hovering over her and thought she recognized Caspar.

Their anger, however, turned quickly into something resembling good humour. Their punches and kicks became a source of entertainment and soon they began to take turns climbing onto a pew and jumping on her back. Most fell short, or fell onto her legs, as Anna tried desperately to crawl away, feeling her fingernails grate against the stone floor of the church. When she realized this was impossible, she turned over and managed to kick out, colliding with a body.

'That hu-uu-rts!' a girl wheezed, unable to catch her breath.

This seemed to momentarily stun them, and Anna managed to stand up. She knew she wouldn't be able to get away, it would be impossible to outrun them, there were so many.

'Your mothers will hear all about this,' she cried. Her voice was thin and sounded false even to herself. It was something she would have said at the market, if she had seen the children misbehaving out of sight of their parents.

She recognized so many of them. It was absurd to say this now, especially because so many of their mothers were dead. Yet, a small pocket of space formed round her. They almost appeared hopeful, as if they hoped their mothers would show up any minute and chastise them. They had no idea what they had done, the permanency of their actions, the situation was totally lost on them. They had yet to wake.

She said it again, but this time with more authority and they retreated a little more. Anna turned round and hobbled quickly towards the doors. Pink and orange sunlight had crested the horizon, and Anna could see her sons far off in the distance, running down the main road towards the river.

# CHAPTER 28

The moment his mother was lost under the throng of children, Konrad had fled from the church with Manfred, pulling him down the steps. Whenever Manfred tried to flop down or raised his arms to be carried, Konrad gripped him even more tightly and dragged him until his legs were forced to move. Without any clear notion of where they were headed, Konrad simply went straight and not until they were beside the river on the tow path, was he forced to stop.

He felt disorientated. His face felt numb and his breathing was rapid and sharp. He eased his grip on Manfred's wrist, eventually letting him go and he dropped where he stood, emitting a simpering whine. Konrad paced in a little circle, his hands pulled at his hair. The image of his mother sinking into violence with so much blood came to him. Everywhere there was blood. His mind closed on what he had just witnessed, and he felt dislodged from reality. A sudden pressing need that they go home now overwhelmed him.

He thought of his meeting with his mother here just the other day, how she had looked when she first came upon him with the sun setting behind her, so her features were in shadow. Then, when she sat down next to him, her face became fully realized both before him and in his memory. He had missed her terribly. When he crawled into her lap, he had savoured all the scents of home that she carried on her dress and in her skin.

He had been so hopeful, that their reunion on the river-bank would have a different outcome than it did. Konrad wanted his mother to see how pious he had become, show her how he had given himself so wholly to God. But it was no use, she only ever wanted Manfred. He looked down at his brother, who was still whining. He was wagging his spoon back and forth at an agitated speed.

If they were to live back at the tavern, he couldn't bear Manfred to continue his charade, his lies. There was no reason to go on pretending any more, no reason to continue covering up the truth.

'You little faker. Things will be different now.' He bent down and came close to his bother's face. Manfred's blue eyes briefly met his own, and Konrad saw that flicker of intelligence he hid so well. Manfred knew exactly what he was doing, what he had done.

Konrad took the spoon. He didn't even bother looking into it, he knew God wasn't there and never had been. He hurled the spoon into the river, and said, 'That's enough.'

Manfred stood, then jumped up and down, waving his hands in front of his chest in protest. It took Konrad a moment to realize he intended to retrieve it. Did he expect the river to part for him? Did he expect to be like Moses? He watched his brother wade in towards where the spoon had dropped through the river's surface. Konrad assumed Manfred would turn round, but he went further into the river. Konrad felt firmly planted where he stood. He couldn't seem to move as he saw his brother go further and further in, until the river reached his chest and he was lifted up by the current and, in what seemed barely a moment, he was swept away.

His mother was suddenly by his side. She rushed past him and into the river up to her waist. She called out for Manfred in deep guttural screams. He noticed blood on her hands. As they went in and out of the water, the blood turned a pale pink that matched the colour of the river's surface and he thought, isn't that funny, you would think the river was pink if you didn't know better.

She got out of the water and ran up and down the riverbank, continuing to call out for her son. It was only when she had been reduced to a staggering gait and bumped into Konrad that she seemed to notice he was there. She grabbed his shoulders and violently shook him.

'What did you do? What did you do?'

Finally she dropped to her knees and fell onto her side, her arms wrapped round herself, her eyes wide open looking straight up. Though Konrad could see the ragged rise and fall of her chest, she looked dead.

He turned and ran away from her. He ran until his heart pounded in his chest as if wanting to escape. He ran all the way up the tow path and under the bridge that was usually guarded. But if a guard saw him, he didn't stop him, or ask where he was going. Perhaps they were relieved for the city to have one less child. He ran until the city itself was behind him and the sun had made its arcing path in the sky. He ran until his body shed any traces of childishness. He ran until he wandered the earth like Cain, until the scene by the river became an obscure and distant memory buried by the passing years.

He ran.

# CHAPTER 29

Light hit the river's corrugated surface in a way that made it seem as though a thousand golden spoons were afloat above him. It was as if his spoon had multiplied infinitely and yet when he frantically tried reaching up for one and then another and another, he never managed to get hold of a single spoon. Then the most miraculous thing happened. The spoons came loose from the water's surface and, still glinting with light, they swam next to him, occasionally bumping into him like a school of iridescent fish. As he rolled along in the current, all the spoons followed him, and those in front moved this way and that, avoiding passing debris and weeds that emitted their own glowing auras. Drifting silt seemed effervescent and the murky clouds of loosened sediment also became imbued with the same luminosity of the spoons, and so appeared celebratory like a continuous sequence of fireworks. He felt exquisitely weightless and bright like vapour on a window on a sunny day.

And so Manfred died at the centre of this pageantry of light.

His body would finally become entangled on the exposed roots of an ash tree where the bank had eroded. He was discovered by early evening. Because his death corresponded with the simultaneous recovery of all the children in the wake-house, Manfred would be declared a saint only weeks after his death. It was generally accepted that Father Gottlieb simply tripped while running and accidentally stabbed himself. Why he had a knife in the first place was a puzzle but insignificant. It was only important that the witch-panic was over, and the children were released from the wake-house, some bound for home, many others for orphanages. There was support for the notion that the children themselves had caused Father Gottlieb's death after they had started to dream of him there at the sabbat, and he was revealed to be an anti-Christ. The wolf in sheep's clothing. In the brief investigation that ensued, some of the children, when questioned, even admitted to it and, for some, this made it easier to accept their children back into their home.

A statue of Manfred was soon erected under the ash tree. The spoon that was the symbol representing Manfred's life would remain for ever fixed in his hand. Yearly mass pilgrimages were made to his statue. Manfred was now known as the patron saint of the ailing, of fair weather and good crops.

Afterwards, pilgrims could purchase a small spoon hanging from a leather strip in the market and wear it round their necks.

For the duration of their stay, the pilgrims always took their wine at Manfred's birthplace, which had now been renamed, the Ash Tree tavern.

Anna went to her son's shrine each and every dusk and lit candles at his feet and this, it was said, prevented devilish malevolence from ever re-entering the city.

The name of Anna Wirth became synonymous with maternal devotion.

# EPILOGUE

Earlier, I noticed a light coming in through the rectory window, it formed a square on the opposite wall, framing the undulating shadows of tree branches. I watched it for a long while, in awe of its simple beauty, and it was one of those moments, which I am increasingly experiencing, where I feel I can nearly imagine how your mind worked.

I watched it until it dissolved under the waning evening light, and I felt assured of the journey I am about to take tomorrow, and the other greater journey that is not far off now. I wonder if Mother is there with you, and if she felt my absence through the years as well and if she does now.

I've often imagined you looking down on me in such moments. I wonder if what I have done with my life has in any way, been penance enough for cutting off your earthly life so young. Most often I lament that no accumulation of good deeds could earn such compensation.

313

It must be quite a surprise to see me as an old man. If you do ever look in on me, I know sometimes even I am taken aback when coming across my reflection, yet I have always welcomed ageing. Childhood seemed but a single day, and for this I have always been thankful. I wonder too what you would have looked like. Would you have retained your ethereal beauty as a man? I like to think your beauty would have been subdued by the passing years and replaced with a quiet strength.

It's a wonder, isn't it, that in this new enlightened era, witches have largely been relegated to figments of children's imaginations and only borne in simple minds where logic is immature. Of course a witch occasionally surfaces in small villages, but in large developed cities witch accusations are rare and, when an arrest does occur, it is always met with a wealth of protest. Panics have been prevented by a heavy onslaught of bureaucratic hurdles. In this time of reason, it is increasingly accepted that man does well enough on his own when it comes to committing evil. The devil need not seduce him. Not that this should be reassuring, but at least the slow acceptance of this fact, betters the odds that only the unlawful will suffer the decree of secular law and the innocent will not. I've wondered what others from the wake-house think of this, or how they've lived their lives; how they lived with it. But memory has a forgiving nature; this I think is one of God's greatest demonstrations of His love for us.

314

I think of Father Gottlieb more than I care to, and almost always when I receive confession. I can see how he would have wanted to prevent the very seeds of sin from settling in the most fertile of ground. A child's malleability is such a curious thing, in and of itself. I hear such desperation in my parishioners at times who want to do away with sinful urges that will never let them alone, and I think of how wonderful it would be if that urge never entered one's mind or heart at all. How I wish the very first signs of sinful impulses could be plucked from a child's mind before they ever settled, before sinful thoughts become a preoccupation that hinders one's worship of God, or worse, when such thoughts turn into deeds and the sinner's bond with God is broken. It would be the closest to Eden we could ever get.

I suppose this was why I would like to believe Father Gottlieb was motivated by the same reasoning. But perhaps it is the very struggle with our own sinful natures and the triumph over ourselves, and the strain of repentance that allows us to appreciate God so much, and be filled with such love for Him. If it was all so easy, our love might not be so intense. Perhaps I have it wrong, perhaps Father Gottlieb's motives were diabolical or perverted. These things I will know soon enough.

Just as I believe you must know everything now. Why I wrote it this way. Yet I still worry that my motives might be mistaken. I meant it as a way to distance myself from my horrible actions. To be able to tell the truth so brutally, I

315

needed to reanimate my younger self as if he were someone else. I thought I risked dishonesty any other way.

I loved you more in death than in life, and for this I am sorry. I am sorry for all of it, and so I make my dying pilgrimage to you. I will leave this final confession at your feet, and I beseech you to take it to God and let Him pass final judgement on me.

Your loving brother
April 1720
Church of St Michael,
Emsland, Lower Saxony

# Author's Note

Although a work of fiction, this novel was inspired by the true historical events in Esslingen in Germany and in Sweden during the seventeenth century.

In Esslingen a witch panic was instigated by a homosexual affair between two adolescent males. The trials took place between 1662 and 1665 under the guidance of Chief Justice Daniel Hauff who oversaw them and who had an obsessive preoccupation with adolescent sexual deviancy that included homosexuality, incest and bestiality. The trials only ended upon Daniel Hauff's sudden and mysterious death in 1665. It has been speculated that he was murdered by poison. No further witch trials took place in the area after his death.

In Sweden a witch persecution occurred during the years 1668 and 1676 and was based almost entirely on the testimony of children who claimed their souls were being taken against their will at night by witches and brought to the sabbat. The children were grouped together in special houses where they prayed through the night to prevent their abduction. This encouraged their role as accusers, providing a fertile ground for shared juvenile fantasy, not to mention heightening their susceptibility to suggestion. When the trials ended over 300 people had been executed.

It should be mentioned that both Esslingen and Sweden were Protestant territories.

The following is a short list of books that helped me in my research:

Bengt, Ankarloo and Clark, Stuart (ed.), *Witchcraft and Magic in Europe*, vol. 4, University of Pennsylvania Press, 2002

Briggs, Robin, *Witches and Neighbours*, Viking Penguin, 1996

Forster, Marc, *Catholic Revival in the Age of the Baroque*, Cambridge University Press, 2001

Heywood, Colin, *A History of Childhood*, Polity Press, 2001

Midelfort, H.C., *Witch Hunting in Southwestern Germany 1562–1684. The Social and Intellectual Foundations*, Stamford University Press, 1972

Ogilvie, Sheilagh (ed.), *Germany: A New Social and Economic History 1630–1800*, vol. II, St Martin's Press, 1996

Oldridge, Darren (ed.), *The Witchcraft Reader*, Routledge, 2002

Roper, Lyndal, *Witch Craze*, Yale University Press, 2004

——, *Oedipus and the Devil*, Routledge, 1994

Tlusty, Ann, *Bacchus and Civic Order: The Culture of Drink in Early Modern Germany*, University Press of Virginia, 2001

Wiesner, Merry, *Gender, Church and State in Early Modern Germany*, Longman Limited, 1998

I am most indebted to Lyndal Roper's brilliant insights into the psychology behind the witch panics and I would strongly recommend her books to anyone wanting to better understand the witch-hunts. In my opinion they are the best books around on the subject.

I am also eternally grateful for Ann Tlusty's vivid examination of tavern life in early modern Germany, which inspired and guided the tavern in this book.

# Acknowledgments

I want to thank my editor, Kate Lyall-Grant, for her insightful suggestions that always make such perfect sense and for her on-going guidance and support. Immense gratitude is extended to Ann Tlusty for answering an anonymous email and thereafter generously sharing her vast knowledge on seventeenth-century Germany throughout the course of writing this novel. Special thanks to Tara Nicholson, for reading early drafts and offering her sage advice, and never faltering in her support. Many thanks as well to Sherry Graham for being such an enthusiastic reader, and also Scott Smith, Lisa Rasmussen and Scott and Terry Nicholson, as well as the Helen Heller Agency and the Marsh Agency. I also write this acknowledgment with loving memories of my nan, Marie Smith.